FORGOTTEN
FIRSTS

DANIEL SMITH

FORGOTTEN FIRSTS

A COMPENDIUM OF LOST PIONEERS, TREND-SETTERS AND INNOVATORS

JOHN BLAKE

Published by Metro Publishing
an imprint of John Blake Publishing Ltd
3 Bramber Court, 2 Bramber Road,
London W14 9PB, England

www.johnblakepublishing.co.uk

First published in hardback in 2010

ISBN: 978 1 84358 262 5

British Library Cataloguing-in-Publication Data:

A catalogue record for this book is available from the British Library.

Design by www.envydesign.co.uk

Printed in the UK by CPI Mackays, Chatham, ME5 8TD

1 3 5 7 9 10 8 6 4 2

© Text copyright Daniel Smith 2010
Illustrations © Mike Mosedale

Papers used by John Blake Publishing are natural, recyclable products
made from wood grown in sustainable forests. The manufacturing
processes conform to the environmental regulations of the country
of origin.

For Rosie

Acknowledgements

I owe sincere thanks to a number of people who helped me during the writing of this book. First, to Michelle Signore and the team at John Blake Publishing for all their hard work in turning my dog-eared manuscript into what you now hold in your hands. As ever, thanks to my family for their ideas and encouragement, and to Rosie, who was with me when I had the idea for this book and is always first in the queue offering support, enthusiasm and so much else beside. Finally, I must pay tribute to all the incredible people whose lives are detailed across the following pages (apart from the small assortment of murderers and other serious sinners!), for without them this book would consist only of blank pages. If you enjoy it, each of them has played their part; if you don't, alas the buck stops with me.

Contents

FOOD AND DRINK

BUILDINGS AND CONSTRUCTIONS

SCIENCE AND MEDICINE

THE COMMERCIAL WORLD

SPORT

THE SOCIAL FABRIC

ENTERTAINMENT

POLITICS, LAW AND ORDER

A FINAL MISCELLANY

Introduction

I should perhaps begin with a warning. Please do not expect to find within these pages the tales of the classic 'firsts' that everyone knows about. This is not the place to recount the tales of the first man on the moon (Neil Armstrong), the first surgeon to carry out a heart transplant (Dr Christiaan Barnard) or the first 'talkie' movie (*The Jazz Singer*). Those stories and others like them are worthy of retelling but, thankfully, there are those who are doing just that. This book is rather more concerned with the untold stories of people (both good and bad) and events that have helped shape the world we live in today.

The idea for this collection first came about over a bowl of soup in a café in the middle of Dublin sometime in early 2008. I found myself somewhat unexpectedly ushered up to a makeshift theatre on the top floor to watch a one-woman play while supping my way through some minestrone. The show was written and acted by Lynda Radley, and it was about a character she had stumbled across in an old photograph. The subject was Mercedes Gleitze, an extraordinary woman who, among many other achievements, was the first British woman to swim the Channel. Though that is not even half the story, as you will be able to see in the entry on page 153.

Radley's performance was in part about remembering an incredible life that had been all but forgotten. And that got me thinking. We live in a very strange age where our lives can seemingly be thrown off kilter by news of the latest shopping purchase or cream-cake consumption or unexpected bout of flatulence of some apparent celebrity or other. As a society, we spend an awful lot of energy being concerned about the banal goings-on of unremarkable people. And yet we happily consign to the filing cabinet of history so many wonderful stories of exceptional (and sometimes peculiar) characters and events, scarcely giving them a second thought.

So after the show I undertook some research of my own into the amazing Miss Gleitze and discovered somebody who really does deserve to be more than a footnote in our collective history, because she was a person who truly *lived* a life. And she, of course, is but one of many. Indeed, in some ways, her 'first' is not among the most striking contained herein. She was not the first person to swim the Channel, or even the first woman. She was 'merely' the first British woman to do it. But, if it wasn't for her, then this book would never have happened, and so she rightfully takes her place within it.

Henry David Thoreau, the great nineteenth-century American writer, philosopher and activist, knew the worth of somebody prepared to trailblaze their own path. He wrote, 'If a man does not keep pace with his companions, perhaps it is because he hears a different drummer. Let him step to the music which he hears, however measured or far away.'

Of course, a small volume such as this cannot begin to redress the balance for all those forgotten innovators and originals. It is simply a motley smorgasbord of a hundred and one of those great forgottens, and its principal aim is to whet the appetite. I hope that this book will afford a few of them the recognition they deserve, but most of all I hope that their stories will entertain and fascinate.

'Where the hell is my world map?'

CHAPTER ONE

The Arts and Culture

The First Opera Composer: Jacopo Peri

Opera emerged out of the neoclassical desire to reconstruct what its leading lights believed (or rather guessed) was the theatrical experience as it was understood in ancient Greece. Florence under the Medici dynasty was, of course, at the heart of all things renaissance and it was here that *Dafne*, regarded as the first opera, was performed in 1597. Its composer was Jacopo Peri, who enlisted the famed poet Ottavio Rinuccini to write the lyrics, or *libretto*.

Peri was born in Rome on 20 August 1561 and undertook formal training as a musician under Cristofor Malvezzi of Lucca. He quickly won renown as a singer and organist before ever winning recognition for his composition skills. He eventually became *maestro di capella* at the Medici court in Florence, serving the Dukes of Tuscany, Ferdinand I and Cosimo II.

In the 1580s, an influential group of humanist thinkers known as the Camerata had prospered in Florence, arguing for the superiority of ancient Roman and Greek culture. Without an awful lot of basis, they had proposed the idea that the chorus in Greek tragedy had been sung, rather than spoken or chanted as was generally thought. It was an idea that much appealed to our composer as well as one of the great Florentine patrons of the arts, Jacopo Corsi, with whom Peri grew close.

Peri probably started composing *Dafne* sometime around 1594 and spent three years working on it. The contribution that Corsi himself made to the piece is unclear, but he was at the very least an important sounding board. The music was composed for harpsichord, lute, viol and flute, while the story tells of Apollo falling in love with the nymph Dafne, who is turned into a laurel in a bid to escape his attentions.

It received its world premiere in front of a privately invited audience at the Palazzo Corsi in Florence, and word spread quickly so that other performances were arranged to meet demand. Unfortunately, Peri's score failed to find its way down to us, although the libretto still exists. While opinion seems to suggest that the music dated rather quickly, Peri and Rinuccini were quite sure of its greatness. Rinuccini noted that his words 'gave pleasure beyond belief to the few who heard it' while Peri said his pioneering music had 'a harmony surpassing that of ordinary speech, but falling so far below the melody of song as to take an intermediate form'.

Regardless of their own thoughts, they did enough to secure a royal commission. The two collaborated on the opera *Euridice*, which was first performed in 1600 at the wedding of Marie de Medici to Henry IV of France. Peri continued to prosper until his death in 1633. While *Dafne* may have failed as an attempt to recreate something of the past, it ushered in a new art form that has prospered for the subsequent four hundred years.

The First Newspaper Editor: Johann Carolus

Since ancient times, the written word has been used to disseminate news, but, historically, news sheets were created on one-off bases to deal with a particular story at a time. Single-story news pamphlets were awash throughout Europe by the fifteenth century. However, the notion of a newspaper with its own identity, publishing regularly and covering a wide range of stories is relatively new. The earliest documented newspaper, as recognised by the World Association of Newspapers, was the not entirely snappily titled *Relation aller Fürnemmen und gedenckwürdigen Historien*. It was first published in German from a press in Strasbourg by Johann Carolus in 1605, its title translating as *The Collection of All Distinguished and Commemorable News*.

By then, Carolus had been producing handwritten news sheets for several years in Strasbourg, which was a Free Imperial City within the Holy Roman Empire. He had built up a network of contacts throughout the region who, for a fee, would provide him with details of all the latest goings-on. Carolus would then sell on his newsletters to a readership of rich clients. However, despite his clientele paying high prices for the most up-to-date gossip and intelligence, the process of producing all those documents by hand was an arduous one, and so he began to think of ways to improve efficiency.

The year 1604 saw the death of one of the most famous print men in the city, Thomas Jobin. Carolus recognised an opportunity and struck up a deal with Jobin's widow to buy the dead man's complete print studio and have it moved wholesale to his own premises for what was, in his own words, 'no little expense'. But now he had the potential to cut his overhead costs and to reach a previously unthinkable new audience. During the summer of 1605, the first copies of *Relation* rolled off the press.

To the modern eye, *Relation* had many characteristics of a book, being of a comparable size, having a full title page and text on each page appearing in a single column. It was nonetheless a success from the outset, as within a few months Carolus was forced to appeal to the Strasbourg authorities for assistance against other printers plagiarising his work. In fact, it is this plea, found buried deep in the Strasbourg archives, that confirms that the paper was up and running by 1605. The oldest edition to have survived until today was not printed until 1609.

The First Fashion Model: Marie Vernet Worth

Marie Augustine Vernet was born on 23 August 1825 in Clermont-Ferrand, France. As a young woman, she found work in Paris, where she would become the wife and muse of Charles Frederick Worth, a man often cited as 'the first couturier'. Worth employed his handsome spouse as a model for his elegant designs and Marie contributed much to his commercial success.

Worth, who was a few months younger than Marie, was born in Lincolnshire and had begun his working life as a textile trader in London. In the mid-1840s, he moved to Paris, finding work with the prestigious drapers Gagelin. It just so happened that Marie was also working for the company at that time.

Sure enough, Worth soon had his head turned by the comely young French girl. By 1850, he was using her as a 'human mannequin' to demonstrate bonnets, shawls and accessories for the shop's wealthy clientele. In June 1851, the couple were married, and Worth, who had long been interested in designing, began to create simple but memorable dresses for her. Before long, the Gagelin customer base were requesting copies to wear themselves.

With the restoration of Napoleon III in the 1850s, Paris was once again the centre of European style. Worth was convinced that Gagelin should branch out into dress-making but its conservative owners were not so sure. A compromise was reached whereby in 1858 Worth was able to strike out on his own, setting up shop on the rue de la Paix with the backing of a rich Swede, Otto Bobergh.

He then set about changing the fashion landscape. At first Marie would visit potential clients to model clothes in their own homes. Worth's brilliant understanding of the female form, his relatively unfussy cuts and his use of rich fabrics won him many fans, including Napoleon's wife, Empress Eugénie. Soon Marie did not have to go out to tout for business. Instead, clients visited the shop and several times a year she and several other models would put on a themed parade of her husband's creations.

Where previously a woman would have approached Worth with an idea for a dress design, they now picked from the modelled garments, which were then altered to their particular requirements. He was also the first major designer to label his clothes. Before long, the fashion house's customer list included stars of the day like Jenny Lind, Lily Langtry, Nelly Melba and Sarah Bernhardt (with Marie personally responsible for winning the patronage of Princess Pauline von Metternich). Sadly, though, Marie was to succumb to a severe bout of bronchitis that brought an end to her modelling career in 1865.

The First Poet Laureate: Gulielmus Peregrinus

The post of Poet Laureate was not formally created until Charles II reclaimed the English throne and honoured John Dryden with the title in 1670, along with an annual pension of £300 and a butt of wine. In return, he was expected to write verse to commemorate important events in the life of the king and the nation. Dryden also became the only poet to be stripped of the title when in 1668 he would not swear allegiance to the Protestant William of Orange on religious grounds.

However, if we are to consider the post as that of 'poet by royal appointment', Dryden was only one in a long and distinguished line that had already included the likes of Ben Jonson, Edmund Spenser and Geoffrey Chaucer. The first in that line was a poet whose name and works have kept rather less well through the ages. His name was Gulielmus Peregrinus and he was the *versificator Regis* (that is to say, the King's Poet) of Richard I, the Lion Heart. We have precious little information about his life and none of his works has come down to us. What we do know of him comes only from mentions here and there in the works of others. Referred to variously as Gulielmus de Canno and as William the Pilgrime, he was a much admired exponent of epic verse and was appointed the king's man sometime around 1190.

Among our best sources about him is *The Principal Navigations, Voyages, Traffiques and Discoveries of the English Nation*, written by Richard Hakluyt at the end of the sixteenth century – long after Gulielmus had thrown off his mortal coil. Hakluyt confirms that the poet was English-born and was 'a very excellent Poet ... of great fame'. Gulielmus was a close observer of the king in the build-up to his crusade 'against the Saracens', on which he embarked in the summer of 1190, and accompanied him during adventures on the Spanish Seas, in Palestine and Syria, and in his encounters 'against the Sultan King of Babylon'. Armed with this wealth of raw material to stoke his creativity, he composed an epic 'in lively colours' that he called

The Expedition of King Richard (a title that probably did not represent his lyrical peak), which was dedicated to the Archbishop of Canterbury and to one of the king's favoured courtiers, Stephen Turneham.

Richard the Lion Heart died in 1199 but Gulielmus seemingly retained his position under the new king, John, until his own death around 1207. He is said to have flourished and prospered in these later years and it is to be much regretted that none of his own work remains to speak on his behalf.

The First Ballet: *Le Ballet Comique de la Reine*

For some, ballet represents the zenith of high culture; for others, it is but a ragtag of people prancing around in tights. Whatever your own particular take, the entertainment considered to have been the original ballet was *Le Ballet Comique de la Reine*, which was performed in 1581 at the Parisian royal court, then still heavily under the Italian court influences of the widowed Queen Consort Catherine de Medici. Although the first 'ballet dancers' had appeared in Italy in the fifteenth century (the word coming from the Italian '*ballo*', meaning 'dance'), they were really exponents of traditional court dancing. What was staged in 1581 was several leaps and pirouettes on from that.

The world premiere took place in front of an audience

said to be in excess of ten thousand on Sunday, 15 October, running from ten o'clock at night until three o'clock in the morning. The exact location is disputed but it was either in the Grand Salle of the Louvre or at the Salle de Bourbon of the Petit Palais. The work was commissioned by Louise, wife of Henri III of France, as a celebration of the wedding of her sister, Marguerite de Lorraine, to Anne (despite the name, the decidedly male Duke of Joyeuse). The man to whom Louise turned to create the piece was one Balthasar de Beaujoyeulx, who immediately went into self-imposed seclusion on receiving his instructions.

After a period of contemplation he re-emerged to demand that the Queen support him in the project by signing up the best talent available. Lambert de Beaulieu was charged with composing the music while Jacques Salmon, Master of the King's Musicians, was to oversee performance. The libretto, based on the ancient Greek myth of Circe, was to be written by the Sieur de la Chesnaye (the King's poet) and the monarch's favoured painter, Jacques Patin, was put in charge of the set design.

The story of Circe came from Homer's *Odyssey* and concerned the eponymous goddess's attempts to use her magic to entrap Odysseus and his men and turn them into animals. The ballet version added the subtle twist of a showdown with the ultimately triumphant king of

France. Beaujoyeulx choreographed the piece, mining the rich traditions of courtly dance to help tell the tale. It was this use of dance as part of the narrative, rather than in its traditional role as incidental to the action, that marked out the production as a turning point in Western culture. With dozens of dancers appearing on stage at a time, this was a revolutionary new attempt to combine music, poetry, dance, costume and staging into a consciously coherent 'piece'.

The performance was a triumph (if rather on the long side, coming in at over five hours) and wowed the Valois court. Beaujoyeulx himself was pleased, too. Never one for knowingly underselling himself, he noted that '... within a single well-proportioned body I have pleased eye, ear and mind'.

The First Datable Printed Book:
The Diamond Sutra

The oldest known form of printing, initially on textiles and later on paper, was via the use of engraved woodblocks, a system first developed in ancient East Asia. The oldest known printed book that can be accurately dated is the *Diamond Sutra*, a Buddhist text dating back to AD 868.

Sutras are Buddhist scriptures and the *Diamond Sutra*, taught by Buddha to his disciple Subhuti, deals with the philosophical concept of non-abidance. Towards the end of the text, Subhuti is instructed to call it 'The Diamond of Transcendent Wisdom', hence its name today.

A colophon – a note at the end of the text – on the printed edition in question reads, 'Reverently made for universal distribution by Wang Jie on behalf of his two parents on the 13th of the 4th moon of the 9th year of Xiantong' (which is to say, 11 May 868). It was printed on seven separate sheets, one of which is an illustration showing Buddha surrounded by disciples and a couple of cats. The sheets were then attached to form a scroll over 15 feet long.

It would seem that the *Diamond Sutra* was printed at Dunhuang, a walled city that prospered because of its location on the Silk Road. An important centre of Buddhism, around 1127, it was subjected to raids from a nomadic group called the His-hsia. It was at this stage that persons unknown stored the *Sutra*, and a great many other works, in nearby caves that have come to be known as the Thousand Buddha network.

The stockpile was then forgotten about for many hundreds of years and was only rediscovered in 1900 by a monk, Wang Yuan-lu. As he explored the caves, he came across the collection of more than 10,000 works of art and literature. In 1907, the area was visited by a British explorer, Sir Aurel Stein, who struck a deal with the monk to buy two dozen cases of material for £130. Among his hoard was the ancient *Sutra*, which now resides (to Beijing's continuing chagrin) in the British Library in London.

In 1966, at the Bulguska Temple in Korea, another printed manuscript, known as the *Great Dharani Sutra*, was discovered in its reliquary. Analysis of the material and of the language used point to its predating even the *Diamond Sutra*, with leading academics believing it must have been printed by AD 705. However, a definite date is yet to be attributed and the work is a miniature, ensuring the *Diamond Sutra* retains its position in publishing history.

The First Regular Newspaper Cartoon Strip: *The Yellow Kid*

The Yellow Kid was a bald, plug-eared, buck-toothed grotesque from the wrong side of New York's tracks. He seemed an unlikely prospect to become a money-spinning cultural icon, but that is just what happened when he became the star of the world's first regular newspaper cartoon strip.

The Yellow Kid was the name by which everybody knew Mickey Dugan, a character created by Richard F. Outcault. Outcault was born in Ohio in 1863 and he attended McMicken University's School of Design in

Cincinnati. After graduating he got a job as an artist with Thomas Edison's company that saw him posted to Paris for a period. He came to New York around 1890 and started touting his cartoons around several of the city's leading magazines.

In 1894, he had a piece accepted in Joseph Pulitzer's *New York World*, a jokey parody of Darwin's *On the Origin of Species* that involved a snake eating a dog and turning into a crocodile. It was well received, and on the back of it the magazine agreed to take a strip from Outcault called *Down Hogan's Alley* (later renamed simply *Hogan's Alley*), which had already debuted in *Truth* magazine. Set in a slum neighbourhood, it revolved around a cast of black and Irish-American street kids and passed occasionally scathing comment on American middle-class attitudes to the poor. The first strip appeared in *New York World* on 17 February 1895. The Kid began as just one of the gang, dressed in a trademark nightshirt that was often adorned with words reflecting the character's inner thoughts. The garment was initially rendered in black and white and later in pale blue, and it took several months before it turned yellow, thus birthing the Yellow Kid proper.

The cartoon was an immediate hit and the Yellow Kid emerged as its star turn. From an appearance once a week, he was soon in the paper more days than not. Before long came the marketing deals, with the Kid advertising products as varied as soap, whisky, cigarettes, buttons and chewing gum. There were even theatrical shows created to cash in on his popularity. As Outcault himself noted, 'The Yellow Kid was not an individual but a type ... I would encounter him often, wandering out of doorways or sitting down on dirty doorsteps. I always loved the Kid. He had a sweet character and a sunny disposition, and was generous to a fault.'

At almost the same time, the great media magnate William Randolph Hearst had bought a rival New York publication, the *New York Journal*. There was an almighty circulation battle between Hearst and Pulitzer, with both men well aware of the power that Outcault wielded. He took full advantage, moving between the papers as the financial offers dictated, before finally plumping for Hearst's *Journal*.

This led to a curious situation. Because of a hazy copyright situation, Outcault drew *The Yellow Kid* for Hearst while Pulitzer employed another cartoonist, George Lukz, to continue *Hogan's Alley*, complete with the Kid. So it was that, for almost two years, the great rivals ran competing strips featuring the Yellow Kid. It was from this scenario that we come to have the phrase 'yellow journalism', to mean journalism more interested in sensationalism and profit than journalistic integrity.

Despite coming out of the affair very well financially, Outcault tired of the legal back-and-forth and the damage to his own reputation. He decided to end the strip, with the last cartoon published on 6 February 1898. He subsequently left the Hearst empire and created several other hugely successful strips, including *Buster Brown*, *Kelly's Kids* and *Buddy Tucker*. The unprecedented success of *The Yellow Kid* saw the introduction of regular comic strips into newspapers throughout the world, a trend that continues even amid the multimedia bonanza on offer in the twenty-first century.

The First Cartographer to Produce a World Map: Anaximander

Anaximander was born sometime between 612 and 610 BC in Miletus on the Ionian coast of Anatolia (Asia Minor). The city was a great cradle of philosophy, producing, among others, the mathematician, astronomer, engineer and politician Thales. Sometimes called 'the first philosopher', Thales attempted to find natural explanations for the workings of the world, notably concluding that the Earth was afloat, like a raft on water. (Even great minds can't be right all the time.)

Anaximander was a student and disciple of Thales and, indeed, is regarded as the second great philosopher of ancient Greece. Few fragments of his writings remain and we know little of his character, although it was said that he could be rather solemn and was prone to pompous dress. He was a man who sought rational, physical explanations to the big questions of the universe and was unafraid to question ancient myths and the idea of the gods themselves. Pursuing his radical trains of thought and questioning the belief in governing supernatural powers, he became a pioneer of the sciences of meteorology, geography, astronomy and cartography.

Perhaps his most lasting theory is that of the apeiron, which argues for an 'Infinite' or 'Boundless' from which everything else emerges and to which everything eventually returns. He believed that the Earth was disc-shaped (with humans dwelling on its flattened top) and surrounded by mist and a wall of fire. Driven by remarkable intellect and imagination, Anaximander was the first human we have record of to attempt to map the complete known world, which he inscribed on a tablet.

With his distinctly unorthodox worldview, allied to the fact that only a very small section of the Earth's surface had come to the attention of the ancient Anatolians, his map was of course rather different from anything that we have today. Sadly, it was destroyed far back in the mists of time, but we can deduce a little of its contents from the descriptions of Herodotus and because Hecataeus of Miletus produced a map of his own some 50 years later, which he said was an improvised version of Anaximander's original.

Inevitably, Ionia stood at the centre of Anaximander's map, which stretched as far as the Caspian Sea in the east and to the Pillars of Hercules (roughly Gibraltar and Mount Hacho in Morocco) in the west. To the north it reached as far as 'Middle Europe' and to the south down to Ethiopia and the lower Nile region.

It would be easy for the modern observer to regard his attempt disparagingly, but it is worth remembering that Anaximander, reputedly a keen traveller himself, was engaged in expanding mankind's horizons at a time when most people could not envisage reality beyond the physically narrow confines of their everyday world. Where once were tales of distant lands full of mythical peoples and unearthly beasts, Anaximander was the first man to attempt to impose a rational global overview of the Earth.

The First Crime-Fiction Writer:
Steen Steensen Blicher

Far less well known than that other great pioneer of the modern crime-fiction genre, Edgar Allan Poe, is Steen Steensen Blicher, who published his landmark novella *The Rector of Veilbye* in 1829, a good 12 years before Poe came out with *The Murders in the Rue Morgue*. Yet it is Poe who is so often cited as the man who began the amazing rise of crime fiction to its current position as perhaps the single most popular and enduring genre in world literature.

One of the big differences between the two men's works is that, whereas Poe depicted a sleuth of some brilliance in C. Auguste Dupin, Blicher gave the world a fumbling local judge who fails to solve the murder mystery put in front of him. It may be for this reason that Poe's work has remained constantly popular, whereas Blicher is only now starting to receive the acclaim he is surely due.

Blicher was born in 1782 in the Jutland region of Denmark, a landscape that would influence and permeate the literary work he produced throughout his life. After years of teaching and then working on the land, he became a parson in his forties (just as his father had been) in the parish of Spentrup, but it was a career for which he was particularly badly fitted. Married with ten children, he was prone to bouts of melancholy, which he was reputed to have fed with the bottle. Hunting in the wilds and writing were far higher on his list of loves than the Church, and his propensity for run-ins with his clerical superiors did not make things any better.

As well as a talented poet, Blicher is chiefly remembered for his contribution to the development of the Danish short story. While much of what he produced may legitimately be regarded as on the light side, others of his works were mini-masterpieces of psychological insight. *Tardy Awakening*, for instance, is a dark profile of marital deception and tragedy that, it has been suggested, reflected his own domestic situation at the time. Coupled to this intensity was a lilting prose style when he came to describing his beloved homeland.

The Rector of Veilbye is the tale of the eponymous rector who is suspected of a brutal murder. The case is brought to the attention of Erik Sørensen (the local judge and sheriff as well as the rector's prospective son-in-law) by the victim's brother, a rough character with an existing grudge against the accused.

Told through Sørensen's diary extracts before finishing with a narrative by the rector's successor 20 years after the events described, the story depicts Sørensen struggling to find an alternative solution in the face of apparently indisputable evidence. It can only be wondered whether Blicher took some kind of pleasure in exposing a man of the church to such difficulty, having himself had several run-ins with men of the cloth by then.

To a modern reader, the story may be criticised for its

predictability, but that no doubt reflects the fact that we are now well versed in the rules of the crime story. For a reader coming to it in 1829 ignorant of any such formulas, it must have been a rather shocking read with its elements of gothic horror and its sad conclusion.

Others may have come along and improved on Blicher's blueprint, but the story remains entertaining and readable and set a benchmark for all who followed. In 2006, it was inducted into the Danish Ministry of Culture's *Kulturkanon* as a 'milestone in Denmark's long and complex cultural history'.

The First Recording Artist: Jules Levy

In 1877, Thomas Alva Edison, a man with his fingers in more than his fair share of 'first pies', invented the phonograph. It was in many ways the result of his earlier work in the areas of the telegraph and the telephone that allowed for the first time the recording and reproduction of sound. Though his technology appears rather basic to the modern observer, it was revolutionary at the time. The first phonograph was essentially a whizzing cylinder covered in tin foil, with sound translated into indentations in the foil, allowing the previously impermanent to become everlasting.

It may be argued that Edison himself was the first person to record a song when he performed 'Mary Had a

Little Lamb' to demonstrate his invention. However, for all his many and remarkable talents, musical performance was not high on the list, and this first recording belonged irrefutably to the 'spoken word' genre.

Instead, he turned to Jules Levy, arguably the greatest cornetist of his age. Born in London in 1838, Levy came from humble beginnings. When but a boy, he came into possession of a cornet mouthpiece, which became an almost constant companion to him for five long years while he dreamed of owning a complete instrument. At last his father buckled and bought him one at auction, though it was a cheap and imperfect example. Without formal training, Levy attacked the instrument with such gusto that 'I nearly blew myself into consumption' and was ordered by his doctor not to play for three months.

Eventually, he was taken under the wing of a man called Dan Godfrey, who led a military band and recognised the young man's talents. Levy claimed he practised some 10 or 12 hours a day and the hard work soon began to pay dividends. For a time he found work in the theatres of London, playing incidental music between acts. In 1865, he made his first trip to America, playing the Boston Music Hall. Soon he was in demand at the great concert halls of North America and Europe and, at his peak in the 1870s and 1880s, was billed as 'the world's greatest'.

In 1878, he hooked up with Edison and made what is generally thought to be the first musical recording, a rendition of 'Yankee Doodle'. The relationship between the two men continued and included events where Levy 'duelled' against the new machine. On 22 June 1878, the *Scientific American* ran an article entitled 'The Phonograph Wins a Victory'. In it, the phonograph is praised for its 'remarkably accurate reproductions' of Levy's riffing and how it 'not only follows Levy, but surpasses him by reproducing cornet notes in entirely new octaves of its own origination'. Edison 1 – Levy 0.

Levy went on to record extensively for the Columbia Records and Victor Records labels until his death in Chicago in 1903.

'I think it's just as well you didn't illustrate it.'

CHAPTER TWO

Food and Drink

The First Restaurateur: Monsieur Boulanger

Where there have been hungry mouths to feed, there have always been eateries. We have documentary evidence of flourishing dining cultures in ancient Rome, ancient China, the early Islamic world and medieval England. But it was not until relatively recently, in pre-Revolution France, that the first establishment to go by the name of *restaurant* came into being.

The man responsible was one Monsieur Boulanger – the historical record does not offer a clue as to his first name. What we do know is that Boulanger ran a popular all-night tavern at the junction of the Rue Bailleul and the Rue Pouille (now the Rue de Louvre) in the 1st arrondissement of Paris. Particularly favoured were the rich soups he served, which he called *restaurants* (restoratives).

At the time, French law decreed that cooked meals could be served only in the private residences of members of the Guild of Traiteurs, which ran a highly effective monopoly. Boulanger, though, was not afraid to challenge them. As things stood, his soups were not classified as 'food', so he could sell them freely in his tavern. However, as he developed a growing and faithful clientele, the Guild looked on nervously. They seized on one of his specialities, sheep's feet in white sauce, and declared that this was a full meal, infringed the Guild's legal rights and represented unfair competition. To the benefit of gourmands everywhere, in 1765 their case was thrown out by the courts and Boulanger set up an eating establishment which he called Le Champ-d'Oiseau.

Boulanger seems to have cut quite a figure, taking to the streets in his finest clothes and wearing a sword as he bid for business. The writer Diderot was among his most regular diners, reputedly as attracted to the delectable Madame Boulanger as much as the food, which was served on small marble tables. The sign Boulanger hung above his door read, 'Boulanger débite des restaurants divins' (roughly translated as 'Boulanger provides divine sustenance'). Before long, devotees referred to his tavern as 'the restaurant' and over time the term was applied to other eateries.

The French Revolution was to play an instrumental

role in the spread of the restaurant as we know it today. With the guillotine hard at work throughout the early 1790s, there were significantly fewer aristocratic bellies to fill. The army of skilled cooks and waiting staff that had attended to them were left searching for new work. Many adapted their skills to the needs of the burgeoning new restaurant sector, establishing Paris as the culinary capital of the world.

The First Known Scotch Whisky Distiller: Friar John Cor

Whisky, a cure for so many ills, derives its name from the Gaelic *uisge beatha*, which translates as *aqua vitae* or *water of life*. And, as any good Scotsman will tell you, the finest of all whiskies is Scotch whisky. Actually, scratch that, they'll tell you the *only* whisky is Scotch whisky.

The origins of this particular nectar of the gods is rather cloudy, though (unlike a good malt). It seems likely that the secrets of distilling made it to Scotland sometime around the fifth century AD, probably by monks from Ireland, where St Patrick was said to have introduced the process. Others, however, have suggested that returning Crusaders brought the skills back with them from the East much later. There is certainly no written record of whisky in Scotland until the Exchequer Rolls of 1494–95, during the reign of King

James IV, a renowned fan of the drink. The records for 1 June 1494 include the following observation: 'To Friar John Cor, by order of the King, to make aqua vitae VIII bolls of malt.'

It is possible that whisky was already established to some extent by then as a drink of the poor, although it is unlikely that it was left to mature into the smooth drink we know and love today. It would likely have been very rough on the taste buds and quite possibly dangerous to the constitution, too. In monastic terms, it may well have been regarded more as a medicine than a social drink. According to the Malt Whisky Society, eight bolls is roughly half a metric ton and would have been enough to make around 400 modern bottles.

Friar John's drop was surely a cut above in terms of quality if it was fit for the king. John was a Tironension monk at Lindores Abbey, on the outskirts of Newburgh in Fife. Built in 1191 on the banks of the River Tay, Lindores was an imposing red sandstone monastery with a rich history. It had played host, among others, to William Wallace, shortly after his victory at the Battle of Blackearnside in 1298. The monastery also boasted magnificent fruit orchards, some of whose produce presumably found its way into flavouring its famous spirit, and a free-flowing stream that provided another of the vital ingredients.

Alas, Lindores' greatest days were all but over by the time Friar John was working his magic there. In 1559, it was sacked by the reforming John Knox and his men, leaving it in ruins from which it has never recovered. Indeed, it is likely that the general quality of whisky in the land increased rapidly in the subsequent period as a result of the monks, the most skilled distillers in the land, being thrown out into the wider world and forced to make a living. To that extent, a true whisky connoisseur may feel rather grateful for the dissolution.

The First Person to Breakfast on Cereal:
James Caleb Jackson

Born in 1811 in Onondaga County in New York State, Jackson was a man for whom flamboyance and indulgence were anathema. His legacy to the world was a rather dusty and uninspiring preparation of baked flour chunks that he called Granula. However, it offered a new perspective on healthy breakfasts and paved the way for the creation of a worldwide market that is today worth billions.

Jackson was a farmer until his late twenties and a strong advocate of temperance in all things. At the age of 27, he became the proprietor of a newspaper that campaigned for an end to slavery. Unfortunately, the media mogul suffered recurring ill health and was forced to give up work when just 36 years old. In a bid to find a path back to wellbeing, he took himself off to a water spa, where he experienced something of a miracle cure.

He then devoted himself to the promotion of hydrotherapy – the curing of ailments by water treatments – and undertook a degree in medicine. In 1847, he began running a water spa of his own in Cortland County, New York, and in 1858 relocated to Dansville to take charge of a medical institute called the Our Home Hygienic Institute. He was a huge success there and won a country-wide reputation for the Institute, which he eventually bought and renamed Our Home on the Hillside.

While specialising in water treatments, Our Home also promoted good health via diet. In short, this meant that anything most people might *desire* to consume was off the menu. There was to be no red meat, no alcohol, tea or coffee, and definitely no tobacco. In fact, if it wasn't a fruit, vegetable or grain, it was not welcome at Dansville.

As he sought something more suitable to offer his clients for breakfast than the traditional fry-up or, at best, hot cereals, he hit upon a recipe using wholewheat flour, baked into sheets, broken up and rebaked. It was 1863 when Jackson perfected his recipe for Granula. He packaged it in unappealing blocks, from which chunks were chipped away to be soaked overnight in cold milk so that it might be edible by breakfast time the next morning.

The cold breakfast was upon us and, despite its

unpromising beginnings, found increasing popularity. Those other guardians of public wellbeing through abstinence, the Kellogg Brothers over in Michigan, saw that Jackson was on to something and came up with a remarkably similar cold breakfast cereal of their own. When Jackson took them to task (and to the courts) over their use of the Granula name, they backed down and renamed it Granola.

In the meantime, Jackson oversaw the continuing success of Our Home on the Hillside, which found its fair share of famous fans and became a regular stopping-off point on the American lecture circuit. He handed over responsibility for its day-to-day running to his son and his son's wife in the late 1870s. In 1882, it was ravaged by fire but a new facility, the Jackson Sanatorium, sprang up in its place.

Jackson himself lived until 1895, achieving the grand old age of 84, a not inconsiderable achievement considering how weak his constitution had been as a young man. And, of course, the Kelloggs went on to bigger and better things themselves.

The First Cook Book: *De Re Coquinaria* (*The Art of Cooking*)

Compiled sometime in the fourth or fifth century AD, *De Re Coquinaria* is a collection of Roman recipes, widely attributed to the professional gourmet and glutton Marcus Gavius Apicius. Indeed, 'Apicius' came to be a generic name for cook books.

The man himself lived in Rome in the first century AD, enjoying his greatest days under the rule of Emperor Tiberius. While *De Re Coquinaria* was made up of recipes from a number of ancient sources, it is reasonable to think that he was responsible for perhaps three-fifths of the 500-odd described. The book was divided into ten chapters, taking in the following topics: The Chef; Meat; Garden Produce; Miscellaneous Meals; Peas, Beans & Pulses; Fowl; Gourmet Dishes; Quadrupeds; Seafood; and Other Fish. Virtually everything was covered in a sauce (and usually a fish sauce) and the market in mind was clearly the wealthy upper echelons of Roman society.

Apicius was famed for his exuberance and utter overindulgence when it came to food. While we may regard some present-day Michelin chefs as being rather over the top in their approaches to food, they really have nothing on the greedy Roman. It was said that he once sailed all the way to Libya just to obtain some particularly plump prawns and he popularised a number of delicacies such as camel heels and flamingo tongues. He also bred pigs, which he fed on a diet of figs to ensure their livers were as plump and succulent as possible before dispatching them with a huge overdose of honey wine.

Pliny once commented that Apicius was 'born to enjoy every extravagant luxury that could be contrived'. Pliny's fellow writer, Seneca, said that through his cooking school he had 'defiled the age with his teachings'. One suspects he would have taken that not as an insult so much as a commendation. Alas, as we all know, such a lifestyle comes at a cost and eventually the arch consumer found that he had very little left in the bank. He thus took the decision to end his own life. Some have suggested he achieved his goal by a particularly virulent bout of excessive eating.

His recipes lived on, though, appearing in print (rather than handwritten manuscript) for the first time in 1483. The first English translation, going under the title of *Cookery and Dining in Imperial Rome*, appeared in 1936.

The First Coffee Shop Owners: Hakam and Shams

The coffee shop has always been so much more than simply a place where you can quench your thirst. They have been backdrops for business, forums for political, artistic and intellectual debate, and even cradles of revolution.

The delights of coffee originated in the Horn of Africa, probably in the thirteenth century, and over the next couple of hundred years spread to Yemen, Egypt and Arabia. Europe was to catch on only relatively late. Yet we have to wait until the seventeenth century before there is documentary evidence of the coffee shop, found in the writings of the Ottoman historian Pecevi. He described how a shop was opened around 1554 or 1555 in Constantinople (now Istanbul) by two men, Hakam of Aleppo and Shams, a 'wag' from Damascus (both cities being in modern Syria).

They sold their coffee from a large shop in the Tahtalkala neighbourhood of the city to an exclusively male clientele that encompassed everyone from the great thinkers and politicians to layabouts and no-gooders. Pecevi described how groups as large as 30 would come together to talk or listen to poetry, to read or to play popular games such as chess and backgammon. Customers realised they could have a whale of a time and all at precious little expense to themselves.

So popular a venue was it for the citizens of the city that the men of religion began to worry that it was keeping people away from the mosques. Religious teachers were said to have spread word that terrible things went on in the coffee house and that it was no better than a wine tavern. For a while the muftis even declared coffee to be against the law of the scriptures. But the tide was not to be turned. Indeed, the success of the Tahtalkala shop led to the birth of countless imitators, from one-man bands selling their wares on the quiet down back alleys to bright new shops in other districts of the city. Eventually, the religious leaders gave up their battle and pronounced that the drink could be considered legal.

With the spread of the Ottoman Empire and increasing trade between East and West, coffee soon tickled the taste buds of the European wealthy. It was not long before cities such as Vienna, Paris and Oxford were developing their own coffee-house cultures. Sham and Hakam had obviously known what they were doing, providing not only a caffeine hit but an all-round drinking experience that eventually, or so it seems, took over the planet. Quite what they would have made of the Grande Soya Chocca-Mochachinos and other similarly bewildering concoctions available to the modern drinker is a matter of conjecture.

The First Chocolate Bar Manufacturer:
François-Louis Cailler

It is highly debatable as to whether there is a more popular food in the world today than chocolate, which comes in so many forms that there must be a type to delight virtually everyone. So it is somewhat strange to think that our global addiction has taken hold only in the last couple of hundred years. Among those who must claim a king-sized chunk of the blame is François-Louis Cailler, the first in a long line of distinguished Swiss chocolatiers and the man responsible for the first chocolate bars.

Chocolate was first enjoyed by the pre-Columbian peoples of the Americas, who used ground cacao beans as the basis of drinks. When the New World Europeans got hold of it, they sweetened it up, added milk and made it altogether more suited to the palates of those back on the continent they had left behind.

When Cailler was born in 1796 in Switzerland, Italy was the European capital of chocolate making. As well as drinking the stuff, leading chefs had tentatively started using it in cooking, too, especially in cakes. In the 1790s, a Frenchman called Doret, who was working in Turin, invented a machine that produced a semi-solid chocolate paste ideal for use in the kitchen.

Cailler was a young lad visiting a local fair when he first encountered some visiting Turinese chocolatiers and he fell in love with their produce. He took the brave step of leaving his country of birth to offer his services as an apprentice at the Caffarel factory in Milan, learning the ways of the masters. After four years of hard study, he returned to Switzerland and opened the nation's first chocolate factory in 1819, in Corsier close to the coastal city of Vevey. A second factory followed six years later.

With an eye on improving the industrial processes of chocolate making, he set about ensuring greater efficiency in grinding the cacao beans and sugar by installing a steam-driven water wheel in his factory, along with two granite mill stones. His chocolate paste, blended with vanilla and cinnamon, proved very popular with his local customers. Then he hit upon his greatest discovery. He developed a technique of blending his chocolate so smoothly that it could be set into solid bars, unsweetened and ready for cooking. It was the world's first chocolate bar.

Joseph Fry, the Bristol-based English confectioner, took things on a stage further when he produced the world's first bars of 'eating chocolate' in 1847. As for Cailler, he died in 1852 but his company lived on through his son-in-law, Daniel Peter. The latter, a candle maker originally, worked closely with Henri Nestlé and in 1875 mastered the technology required to combine his factory's chocolate with Nestlé's dried milk to bring the world's first milk chocolate bars to market. Quite a boon for a nation that might otherwise be known only for banking and cuckoo clocks.

The First TV Chef: Marcel Boulestin

Xavier Marcel Boulestin was born in Poitiers in France in 1878. During a childhood and youth dominated by his love of music and the dramatic arts, only a brave man would have backed him to find his greatest success as an ambassador for food. But perhaps his theatrical flair and communication skills, combined with the food know-how seemingly inbred into the French character, led him inevitably to the London studios of the then very young BBC in 1937.

Boulestin's winding road to culinary greatness began in earnest when he was 18 and moved to Bordeaux. With an annuity granted in the will of his dead mother, he signed up as a law student at the city's university, but spent most of his time not nose in book but out at concerts, gaining something of a reputation as a *bon viveur*. In 1899, he did his military service before moving to Paris to work as the secretary of Henri Gauthier-Villars, better known as the author Willy and as the wife of Colette.

Boulestin lived a bohemian life there for a few years but with little notable literary success of his own, despite several titles in print. In 1906, he decided it was time for a change and moved to London, but lapsed into a very similar pattern. Then, in 1911, he opened a boutique interiors store, selling materials sourced from the great European cities for a large profit. However, the onset of the First World War threw a large spanner in the works. He became a translator with the British Expeditionary Force for the war's duration and his attempts to resume life as a successful shop owner afterwards didn't get off the ground.

Then, in 1923, his fortunes took an upswing. He casually suggested to an editor at Heinemann Publishers that he might write a cookery book for him. With a £10 advance in his pocket, the result was *Simple French Cooking for English Homes*. It was a rip-roaring bestseller and did much to demystify the French kitchen for an untrusting British market. Boulestin would write a total of 14 cook books up to 1937. In addition, he opened the much-loved Restaurant Français in Leicester Square in 1925 and the even more legendary Boulestin's Restaurant in Covent Garden two years later.

With his reputation thus established, he was a natural choice when the BBC decided to run an experimental cookery programme in 1937. The first episode of *Cook's Night Out* aired on 21 January at 9.25pm, and Boulestin used his 15 minutes to demonstrate how to cook the perfect omelette. He was well versed in that particular art, having co-written a book entitled *120 Ways of Cooking Eggs*. A further four episodes aired at fortnightly intervals, covering Filet de Sole Murat, Escalope de Veau Choisy, Salads and Crêpes Flambées. The shows were a marked success, despite his not swearing even half as much as Gordon Ramsay.

He went back to France at the outbreak of the Second World War, and was found dead in his Paris flat on 20 September 1943. A *gastronome extraordinaire*, he once observed, 'Cookery is not chemistry. It is an art. It requires instinct and taste rather than exact measurements.' It was a message that effortlessly translated from France to Britain.

'I like it but could we dispense with the toy monkey.'

CHAPTER THREE

Buildings and Constructions

The First Skyscraper: The Home Insurance Building, Chicago

To define what a skyscraper actually is represents quite a challenge, but there is a general acknowledgement that it should fulfil three main criteria: it should be of significant height; it should consist of multiple practicably usable storeys; and it should be built around a self-supporting skeleton.

The title of 'First Skyscraper' is thus a hotly contested one. Some have suggested that an old mill in Shropshire, England, is the legitimate claimant. The Ditherington Flax Mill (also known as the Maltings) was built near Shrewsbury in 1796–97 along the designs of Charles Bage, who used a revolutionary iron frame at its core.

However, it stands about as high as a five-storey building, so, while tall, it is not extraordinarily so.

Other architectural historians have pointed to George Post's Equitable Life Assurance Building, which first rose above the skyline of New York (for many, the spiritual home of the skyscraper) in 1870. It was in many ways the prototype for what we now think of as a skyscraper, soaring an impressive 40 metres (130 feet) into the air on Broadway, with a primitive metal structure helping to support its seven storeys. It was also the first office building to include passenger elevators. Alas, the construction was consumed by a huge fire in 1912.

However, as the first building to meet all criteria and to have 10 storeys (and later, 12), the Home Insurance Building, constructed at the northeast corner of La Salle and Adams in Chicago in 1931, has perhaps the strongest of all claims. Built in 1885 under architect William LeBaron Jenney, it was initially 42 metres (138 feet) high but, after the addition of extra floors in 1890, grew to 55 metres (180 feet).

Jenney had been born into a family of Massachusetts shipbuilders but, having served as an engineer during the Civil War, was practising as an architect by the late 1860s. His training had taken him to Paris, where he was a close contemporary of Gustave Eiffel, who attained everlasting fame through the tower he erected for the 1889 Universal Exposition.

When Jenney drew up his plans for the Home Insurance Building, he used a skeleton of fire-resistant steel and iron to bear the greater part of the load, rather than relying on masonry features. Because of this, the building was estimated to weigh only about 35 per cent of a similarly sized traditional brick-and-stone building. However, it should be noted that more recent academic enquiries suggest the structure made at least some use of traditional masonry to augment the metal frame.

Jenney is considered the founding father of the Chicago School of architecture and his 1891 Manhattan Building, also in Chicago, was the first skyscraper to reach 16 storeys. As for the Home Insurance Building, where Jenney pioneered, many others followed and surpassed. By 1931, the edifice was a relative dwarf in skyscraper terms and it was unceremoniously ripped down to make room for something bigger.

The First Roller Coaster: Les Montagnes Russes à Belleville

Beloved of thrill seekers everywhere, modern roller coasters are magnificent feats of engineering, manipulating the forces of nature to inflict a plethora of disconcerting sensations on the human body and mind. It is, perhaps, slightly surprising, then, that the first roller coasters were not built for thrill-seeking teenagers but for the aristocrats of Napoleonic France.

In fact, the roller coaster's direct ancestors were the famous 'Russian Mountains', huge ice slides that quickened the pulses of the Russian aristocracy around St Petersburg in the 1600s. These wooden constructions could be up to 80 feet high and monied daredevils climbed a flight of stairs before hurtling down a 50-degree incline on a rudimentary sled.

There is talk of a wheeled roller coaster having been built at St Petersburg's Gardens of Oreinbaum in 1784, during the reign of Catherine the Great, but there is a lack of documentary evidence to support the claim. We can, though, be far surer of the existence of Les Montagnes Russes à Belleville (literally, The Russian Mountains of Belleville), which was in operation in Paris by 1817. Employing carriages with wheels fixed into the grooves of a wooden track, this prototype of the roller coasters we know today was developed when attempts to bring the icy magic of the 'Russian Mountains' died amid the much warmer climate of Western Europe. A double track allowed for two carriages to travel side by side in a sort of roller-coaster grand prix, with the intrepid riders achieving speeds of up to 30 miles per hour, before being slowed by deposits of sand at the end of the track.

At the same time, over in the city's Beaujon Gardens, a heart-shaped track called the Promenades Aeriennes was attracting its fair share of attention, sending two carriages at a time in opposite directions from a single central tower. When the vehicles came to rest at ground level, it was the unenviable task of ride attendants to push them manually back up to their starting positions. France's locked-in carriages were significantly safer than the harum-scarum sleds of the 'Russian Mountains', allowing for rides to get higher, steeper and longer. To prove itself the first city of the roller coaster, within a few short years Paris's Frascati Gardens hosted the original ride incorporating a terrifying loop-the-loop.

The First Purpose-Built Cinema: The Vitascope Theater, Buffalo, New York State

In the mid-1890s, the showing of movies for entertainment was in its genesis. In December 1895 in Paris, the Lumière brothers had given what is widely regarded as the world's first public film screening at the Grand Café, but that location was by no stretch of the imagination a 'cinema'. Early the following year, William Rock opened Vitascope Hall on New Orleans'

Canal Street, probably the first venue dedicated to film screening but not a building constructed with that intention in mind (it had originally been a regular retail store).

The Vitascope was an early film projector taken on and promoted with gusto by Thomas Edison's company from around April 1896. Edison had a smooth operation in place, including several 'Edisonia Halls' around the country – spaces which the public could visit to inspect the latest products from the great man and his empire. One such hall was opened at 295 Ellicott Square Building on Buffalo's Main Street by two brothers, Mitchell and Moe Mark. Formerly downtown hatters, they had run the Edisonia Phonograph Parlors at 378 Main Street since 1894, a penny arcade whose amusements included not only phonographs but also Kinetoscopes (which allowed for individuals to enjoy a peepshow) and even X-ray machines. Having moved to the Ellicott Square Building, they made the decision to attach a theatre on to their basement location and opened it to the public on 19 October 1896.

It was, according to contemporary accounts, quite a place, decked out in white and gold, its inclined floor covered with a Wilton carpet. There was a proscenium arch stage, which could be viewed from 72 seats arranged around a central aisle. Deep-maroon hangings adorned the walls and electric lighting added that sense of modernity. Hourly shows ran from 10 in the morning until 11 at night, with films changing every Thursday and Sunday.

The first presentations, mostly productions of the Lumières and later the Pathé brothers, lasted about a minute each and included depictions of various international cities, the coronation of the Russian tsar and, somewhat dubiously, 'two negroes in a watermelon-eating contest'. All tickets cost 10 cents. The theatre could count some 200,000 bottoms on seats in its first year of business and it remained open for around two years.

The Mitchell Brothers proved brilliant cinema operators and soon expanded their operations to New York and Boston. In 1914, they opened a 2,800-seat movie theatre, the Strand, in Manhattan. Designed by Thomas Lamb, it reputedly cost a million dollars to build and was christened the world's first Movie Palace.

The First Doll's House: The Munich Baby House

It is a characteristic of all the best toys that they appeal as much to adults as to the children for whom they were supposedly made. This was certainly the case when in 1558 Albrecht V, Duke of Bavaria, ordered the world's first miniature doll's house for his daughter, Maria Anna, only to decide it was too good for her and keep it for himself. Well done, Dad!

Born in Munich in 1528, Albrecht was something of a hoarder, with particular tastes for Egyptian, Greek and Roman antiquities and for books. His personal collections went on to form the basis of several museums and of the Bavarian state library. It may even have been these fascinations that birthed his idea of a doll's house, as certainly both the Egyptian and Roman cultures had a tradition of 'miniatures', whether of people, creatures or scenes. However, these usually served religious or ceremonial purposes and were far removed from the modern doll's houses, built for pleasure, that we know today.

Whatever the reason, Albrecht requested the construction of one when his daughter, who would later be Archduchess of Austria, was about seven years old. Unfortunately, neither the house nor any drawings of it have come down to us, the model having been destroyed in a fire in the 1670s. However, one of Albrecht's assistants, a man named Johann Baptist Fickler, was good enough to compose a very complete description of the construction and the contents. It does indeed sound like a magnificent dwelling, and on its arrival Albrecht wasted no time in claiming it as its own.

Spreading over four storeys, it had 17 doors and 63 windows. There were several bathrooms, a larder, wine cellar, two kitchens, a ballroom and several parlours and bedrooms, all populated by representations of Maria Anna, her siblings and her mother, Anna. Each room was finished in minute detail, down to exquisite cutlery and crockery, a spit-roasted bird in the kitchen, ivory chamber pots and red silk upholstery. 'Outside' were a garden and several cowsheds.

The house was adored by all those who saw it and started a trend that spread quickly through the upper and middle classes of Europe. Dolls' houses came to be regarded more as status symbols than toys and an industry established itself among the continent's elite furniture designers and makers, giving rise to the production of yet more stunning creations over the next two centuries.

The First Big Wheel Designer: George Ferris

Designed to provide the 'wow factor' at the 1893 World's Columbian Exposition in Chicago, George Ferris's creation has become a staple of theme parks and tourist destinations throughout the world. It provided the iconic setting for one of the greatest scenes in film history, at the end of *The Third Man*, and its descendants, such as the London Eye, are among the most lucrative attractions in the world. All in all, it is quite some legacy for a man whose initial idea was laughed at by his fellow professionals.

Planning began in 1890 for the World's Columbian Exposition, which was to be a celebration of the 400th anniversary of Columbus's discovery of America. Daniel Burnham, one of the up-and-coming architects of the age, was charged with providing the festival with a spectacle to rival the Eiffel Tower, built for Paris's Universal Exposition the previous year. Burnham decided to rile the nation's civil engineers into action, making a speech in which he praised the legacy of America's contemporary architects but cast doubt on the achievements of its engineers.

The initial response was disappointing, with most ideas focused on building a tower that would outstrip Eiffel's. Burnham wanted something entirely new, though. That is when the rather wan and serious-looking Ferris came to the fore. By then in his early thirties, he had graduated as an engineer in 1881. After working for several years on mining and railway projects, he had become senior partner in a firm famed for building steel bridges. It was while there, sometime in the late-1880s, that he had the idea for a giant wheel. The story goes that, following Burnham's speech, he went for dinner with friends and sketched out his idea at the table, a drawing that formed the basis of the final design almost unchanged.

Ferris managed to secure guarantees for $600,000 of funding and approached the Exposition Organizing Committee in 1892 to get the go-ahead to start construction. When fellow industry professionals got wind of the plans, he was widely mocked and came to be known as 'the Man with Wheels in his Head'. Nonetheless, on 16 December 1892, he was given the nod, though the Wheel would be on the Central Avenue grounds rather than the main Jackson Park site.

With only four months until opening day, Ferris appointed the relatively inexperienced Luther Rice to oversee the works, a job made no easier by some ferocious frosts that winter. Yet, on 18 March 1893, the main axle, weighing almost 90,000 pounds and over 45 feet long, arrived from Pittsburgh and was erected within two hours. The Exposition opened on 1 May but the Wheel was not ready for testing until 9 June. Its 36 cars hung, Ferris and his wife went for a test-run on 11 June. Delighted with the results, he nominated 21 June as the day when it would open to the public.

It was an instant success, running without any

engineering problems until the Exposition closed on 6 November. Customers enjoyed one revolution that incorporated six stops, and then a second nonstop revolution lasting nine minutes. On a good day, you could look out over Illinois, Indiana, Michigan and Wisconsin. By the time it had finished its scheduled run, almost one and a half million people had taken a ride at 50 cents a pop.

However, then the story goes awry. It stood *in situ*, useless, for several months before relocation to Lincoln Park. But the magic had gone and the visitors simply didn't arrive. The company Ferris had set up for the project lapsed into debt. Ferris contracted tuberculosis in 1897 and died, not yet 38. The Wheel, crushed with debt, was sold as scrap for just $1,800. It was given the opportunity of a new lease of life in 1904 when it was shipped to Louisiana for another exposition. But the world had moved on and, having barely turned a profit, the Wheel was unceremoniously blown up on 11 May 1906.

The First Lighthouse: The Pharos of Alexandria

Built in the third century BC, this was not only the original lighthouse, it was also one of the Seven Wonders of the World. Built in the period of Hellenistic Egypt, when Greek influence was at its peak, it rose a mighty

140 metres (460 feet) or so above the ground and, it was said, its light was visible for 30 miles out to sea

Pharos was a fairly unremarkable island lying just off the coast of Alexandria, which had been founded as a port city in 332 BC by the legendary Macedonian empire-builder Alexander the Great. When Alexander died in 323 BC, he was succeeded as ruler of Egypt by Ptolemy Soter, and it was he who commissioned plans for the tower that would serve not only as a guide for shipping and a warning to potential enemies, but also as a symbol of the city's greatness. Sadly for Ptolemy Soter, the project was so monumental that it would not be completed until around 270 BC, by which time he had died and his son, Ptolemy Philadelphus, was in power.

The man responsible for designing the building was Sostrates of Knidos and he seized the opportunity to create something magnificent. The Pharos consisted of three major sections. The marble base, the tallest part at some 60 metres (200 feet), was square-shaped and tapered off towards the top. On each corner was a sculpted Triton, the mythological Greek messenger of the Sea. Next came an octagonal section, and that gave way to a circular upper level. This housed a chamber for a burning torch, surrounded by reflective mirrors. As well as providing mariners with something to navigate by, it was said that the setup allowed for light to be concentrated on invading ships so that they caught fire. At the very summit of the tower during the Roman period was a statue of Poseidon, the sea god.

In an episode of outrageous mean-spiritedness, Ptolemy forbade Sostrates from putting his signature on his life's great work, but Sostrates was ultimately to get the better of him. To keep his master sweet, he engraved a tribute to Ptolemy into the stonework on the tower's base. Over the years, though, it wore away to reveal a thick layer of plaster, adorned with the following words: 'Sostrates of Knidos, son of Dexiphanes, to the gods protecting all mariners upon the sea'.

For many centuries one of the tallest buildings on earth (the Great Pyramid of Giza was a little higher), the Pharos was badly damaged by earthquakes in AD 365 and AD 1303. It finally collapsed around 1326, having stood proudly for over a millennium and a half. Such was the fame of the construction that variations of the name 'Pharos' serve as the word for *lighthouse* in several languages, including French (*phare*), Italian and Spanish (*faro*) and Romanian (*far*).

The First Passenger-Carrying Elevator:
The Palace of Versailles

The earliest versions of the elevator, or the lift as we like to call it in Blighty, were designed for transporting goods rather than humans, and were in use in ancient times. Indeed, the great Roman architect and thinker of the first century BC Vitruvius (himself immortalised in Da Vinci's drawing of *Vitruvian Man*) reported that no lesser light than Archimedes had designed a working lift back in the third century BC. His design worked on a system of ropes and pulleys pulled by either horses or men to lift and lower a wooden platform.

But it was to be many centuries before anybody felt confident enough to start moving human cargoes about. The venue was the Palace of Versailles, the grand domicile of the kings of France, and the year was 1743. The motivation was to satisfy the sexual proclivities of the somewhat randy Louis XV. It was called the 'Flying Chair', and the aim was to discreetly manoeuvre the king's lover of the time, the Duchess de Châteauroux, from her apartment on the second floor down to his rooms on the first, or vice versa. The contraption was accessed from an outside balcony and was worked, just like Archimedes' system, by ropes, pulleys and counterweights. These were positioned inside a chimney and could be controlled by a team of men just as soon as the king gave the wink.

In the grand royal tradition, Louis had married a princess, Marie Leszczyńska of Poland, who was more than accommodating in turning a blind eye to his indiscretions. However, even she may have been getting a little 'fromaged off' by the time Marie Anne de Mailly, Duchess de Châteauroux, came on the scene. She was, after all, the third of four sisters who would eventually come to 'know' the king, and was intelligent and stunningly beautiful to boot. Married at 17 to the Marquis de la Tournelle, she was widowed by the age of 23. By that time Louis had had his way with both of her older sisters and now turned his attentions to Marie Anne. At first, she rejected his advances, having her eye on the Duc d'Agénois instead. However, after some court intrigues designed to break her affections in that direction, she succumbed.

Realising an opportunity, she soon won for herself the title of Duchess, got her rivals ousted from the court and ensured she was financially set for life. Unfortunately for her, she had little time left to enjoy on this earth and died suddenly in 1744. Presumably not wanting the 'Flying Chair' to go to waste, Louis soon took Marie Anne's little sister, Diane Adélaïde, to his bed. A short while later, he replaced her with his most famous lover of all, Madame de Pompadour.

Despite the king's making full use of his elevator, it

hardly set a trend. It would not be until the 1850s that the American engineer Elisha Otis invented the safety elevator that could stop itself from plummeting to the ground in the event of a cable breaking. It was a timely invention, coinciding as it did with the beginnings of the age of the skyscraper.

'It's avocado...I distinctly ordered a white bathroom suite.'

CHAPTER FOUR

Science and Medicine

The First Optician: Fra. Alessandro della Spina

For many centuries, and probably millennia, quartz or glass has been crafted into magnifying glasses to aid those suffering from short-sightedness. But it was at best a partial solution, and during the Middle Ages sight loss was a quite devastating condition for many scholars and monks who had spent decades scrutinising aged manuscripts in often awful light. The English friar Roger Bacon was certainly interested in the problem and outlined a theoretical blueprint for glasses in his *Opus Majus* of 1268.

However, the first spectacles as we might recognise them today were invented by a person or persons unknown in the area of Florence/Pisa sometime around 1285. These rivet eyeglasses were, to all intents and purposes, a couple of magnifying glasses with the ends of the handles riveted together so that they could perch on the wearer's nose. We know the rough date of their first appearance from an address made by the Dominican monk Giordano da Rivalto in Florence in February 1306. He noted that 'it is not yet twenty years since there was found the art of making eyeglasses' but did not name the man responsible. For a long while, it was believed that this anonymous inventor was Salvino degl'Armati, whose gravestone read:

Here lies
Salvino d'Armato of the Armati
Of Florence
Inventor of Spectacles
May God forgive him his sins
AD 1317

However, subsequent investigation proved that the gravestone was a much later creation and the claim was a hoax.

So there is little hope that the identity of the first man to make spectacles will ever be known. However, we can be much more confident of the first person to take this most visionary of creations to the masses (or at least to the educated and rich medieval Italian upper classes). He was yet another Dominican Friar, Alessandro della Spina, 'a monk of most excellent character'. A document in the archives of St Catherine's convent in Pisa recorded Alessandro's death in 1313 and elaborated thus:

'When it happened that somebody else was the first to invent eyeglasses and was unwilling to communicate the invention to others, all by himself he made them and good-naturedly shared them with everybody.'

Thus, it would seem that, for reasons best known to himself (no doubt with some financial motivation in mind), the inventor of the spectacles was unwilling to let the world at large share in his achievement. So it fell to a man of God to learn the technology for himself and spread the word of immaculate vision.

The First Sex-Change Case: 'Rudolf' (Dora-R)

The history of gender reassignment is one inevitably shrouded in secrecy, rumour and mythology, and includes many offshoots such as the long-documented existence of eunuchs. However, the first case of an identifiable individual willingly submitting to medical procedures with the intention of 'changing' from one gender to another is that of 'Rudolf', a subject documented by Magnus Hirschfeld, the renowned German sexologist and proprietor of the Berlin Institute for Sexual Science in the first half of the twentieth century.

In 1930, Hirschfeld recorded the story of Rudolf, who had been born sometime around 1890 in Erzgebirge in Germany. When he was about six, it became noticeable that he wished to be dressed like a girl and at the same age he made an unsuccessful attempt to remove his penis by tying string tightly around it. As he went through puberty, his body type had certain feminine characteristics and he continued to practise transvestism, while his 'tendencies were of a homosexual nature'.

At around the age of 26, now living in a large city, he undertook to live his life as a woman. In 1921 he had himself medically castrated but still desired the complete removal of his penis. This was achieved by an operation in 1930 and the subsequent grafting of an artificial vagina. There the history of Rudolf/Dora-R finished.

More famous, though, was the case of the much-lauded Danish Art Deco artist Einer Wegener, who underwent a sex change in 1930, so becoming Lili Elbe. Wegener was another patient of Hirschfeld and received significant press coverage at the time. She was reported dead in 1931, seemingly after her body had rejected transplanted ovaries, although there is speculation that her death was faked in a bid to evade the unwanted attention.

However, widespread public awareness of the sex-change process really came about only in the 1950s, with the case of Christine Jorgensen. Born George Jorgensen in 1926 on the tough streets of the Bronx, the former army man underwent gender-reassignment surgery and hormone treatments in Denmark in the post-war years. In December 1952, the *New York Daily News* ran a headline: 'Ex-GI Becomes Blond Beauty'. Christine coped well with the publicity (in a world a little more ready to accept her than the one that had existed 20 years earlier) and carved out a successful career as an actress, entertainer and campaigner.

The First Man to Build a Modern Water Closet: Sir John Harrington

To the disappointment of schoolboys the world over, the inventor of the modern toilet was not Thomas Crapper. He was but a relatively minor, if successful, designer and manufacturer of toilets who only appeared on the scene in the 1880s, long after modern 'flushing loo' technology was well established. The real 'godfather of the WC' was another Englishman, John Harrington, who went about his business centuries earlier.

John Harrington was born in 1561 and, his mother being an illegitimate daughter of Henry VIII, was a godson of Elizabeth I. Schooled at Eton, he then studied law at Cambridge, though his true strengths lay as a bawdy wit and sometime poet. He established himself as something of a star in the court of Elizabeth, where he was known as her 'saucy godson'.

Until Harrington came on the scene, the favoured toilet type was the somewhat rudimentary 'privy shaft', which was neither hygienic nor particularly seemly. Around 1594, Harrington designed something far improved for installation at his house in Kelston, near Bath in Somerset. His water closet consisted of a pan that was open at the bottom and sealed with a valve. A complex arrangement of levers and counterweights released a powerful rush of water into the bowl at the desired moment. The water served three principal purposes: to flush away the contents of the pan, to clean the bowl and to remove odours. Of course, regular supplies of water were not so readily available then as today, so he recommended flushing at least once a day but, ideally, twice. It was, in his own modest words, a 'privie in perfection'.

Keen to spread the word, Harrington took the brave step of publishing a work about his toilet. *A New Discourse on a Stale Subject, Called the Metamorphosis of Ajax* appeared in 1596 and was on some levels a satirical work about the society in which he lived, but also contained much practical advice on the construction of his water closet. The word Ajax in the title was a pun on the Elizabethan slang term for a toilet, a jakes.

In common with so many innovators working far

ahead of their time, the world at large did not regard Harrington's creation with as much admiration and affection as he did himself. In fact, he became a laughing stock among some in Elizabeth's court, and was reviled by others angered at his libellous allusions. He even fell out of favour with the Queen herself for a while, although she soon came round and requested he fit one of the water closets in her royal palace at Richmond.

Yet she never really took to the new royal throne, particularly disliking the great amount of noise its flushing mechanism made. Instead, the world at large turned their sights towards the chamber pot as the toilet of the future. Elizabeth died in 1603 and Harrington nine years later, but the flush toilet was not to gain common currency until well into the eighteenth century, when its design was significantly improved by engineers including Alexander Cummings and Joseph Bramah.

The First Blood Transfusion Service: The London Blood Transfusion Service

By the early twentieth century, knowledge of blood transfusion was still at a notably primitive stage. Richard Lower, a physician from the University of Oxford, had made strides in the 1660s when he experimented with transfusions from dogs to humans. Meanwhile, Jean Denis, doctor to the French King Louis XIV, was conducting similar animal–human studies at about the same time. However, when one of his patients died and the grieving widow threatened legal action, that particular area of study ground to a halt in both countries. A hundred years later, James Blundell, who worked at Guy's Hospital in London, resurrected the science, but after him there was very little progress until the 1900s. Then, at the beginning of the century, Karl Landsteiner set out the definitive blood-typing system while the use of syringes led to the phasing out of direct donor–patient transfusions.

Yet it was not until 1921 that the first organised blood-transfusion service came into being, thanks to the efforts of Percy Oliver. Born in 1878 in Cornwall, he moved to south London with his parents when he was a young boy. Despite excelling in the entrance exam, Percy was rejected from the civil service on medical grounds but found a role with Camberwell's library service. He also co-founded the local division of the Red Cross, becoming its honorary secretary in 1910.

During the First World War, he signed up with the Royal Naval Air Service and, with his wife, did outstanding work resettling Belgian refugees (for which they were both awarded OBEs). Incidentally, at the outbreak of the war, it was discovered that sodium citrate helped prevent the clotting of blood, paving the way for the eventual introduction of blood banks. However, this administrative development was still some way off when, in 1921, Oliver received his fateful phone call from London's King's College Hospital asking whether he might be able to find a blood donor who could come in person to the hospital urgently.

After a few calls to his Red Cross colleagues, Percy made his way to King's with three companions. Each was tested and one, a Sister Linstead, was selected as a match with the patient. The incident made Percy realise that there was a real need for a roll-call of potential donors who could be called on in an emergency. Working from his home and ably assisted by his wife, he began to establish a London-wide network willing to be called on at any hour of the day or night. Before acceptance on to the scheme, the would-be volunteers were screened to establish their blood type and to ensure they were not infected with syphilis.

In its first year, the London Blood Transfusion Service, as he called it, responded to 13 requests from hospitals. He developed the organisation in partnership with the Red Cross, and within five years it was dealing with 1,300 calls per annum. By the outbreak of the Second World War, Percy's network covered the whole country and could call on 2,700 members to answer 6,000 annual requests for help. By then, Percy had played a key role in the establishment of the Voluntary Blood Donors Association and helped establish guidelines for the appropriate treatment of volunteers. During the war years, he spearheaded the development of a comprehensive national blood bank, which after the war became the National Blood Transfusion Service. He died at St George's Hospital, Westminster, in 1944, the public face of a vital element of public health.

The First Cloned Animals from Laboratory-Cultured Cells: Megan and Morag

After years of sci-fi stories filled with terrifying soulless clones intent on taking over the world, in 1996 came the news that the Roslin Institute in Edinburgh had cloned a sheep, Dolly, from adult somatic cells. Dolly became an instant media sensation as the scientific community raked over the implications of the technological leap, and governments around the world passed legislation prohibiting the development of human cloning.

Dolly was indeed the first mammal to be cloned from laboratory-cultured adult cells, but, a year earlier, two of her cousins, Megan and Morag, had appeared. They were the first mammals to come from laboratory-cultured embryonic cells, yet the fanfare for them was virtually nonexistent.

The Roslin Institute team had set out to develop a

more reliable way of genetically modifying sheep populations. They hit upon a method of taking the nuclei from early-stage embryonic sheep cells and inserting them into unfertilised sheep ova cells that had their own nuclei removed by electrofusion. They were then left to culture *in vitro*, before being placed into potential surrogate mothers.

Some 250 embryos were implanted into unsuspecting Scottish blackface ewes, leading to five live births. However, only Megan and Morag made it past the first ten days. Megan, or Sheep 5LL2, as she was also known, was born on 19 June 1995, with Morag, Sheep 5LL5, following a few days later. Morag, the more forthright and bossy of the sisters, died of lung disease in February 2003 (the same month Dolly died from a similar ailment) and was promptly put on display at the Royal Museum in Edinburgh. Megan, though, was still going strong in 2005, racking up an impressive decade of life.

While the world at large paid scant attention to the emergence of Megan and Morag, the head of the Roslin Institute project, Professor Ian Wilmut, knew just how important a development they represented. He would recall, 'This was our first groundbreaking experiment. After the birth of Megan and Morag, we were confident that one day it would be possible to clone an adult and began to draw up details of just how to do this.'

The First Director of a School for Guide Dogs:
Dr Gerhard Stalling

There are still in existence Roman mosaics dating back to the first century AD which depict dogs leading the blind. Other similar images can be traced in the artworks of subsequent ages, but it seems that there was no formal attempt to train man's best friend in this way on any grand scale until the early nineteenth century. At that point, Johann Wilhelm Klein, the Austrian founder of an Institute for the Education of the Blind, laid out his vision of trained guide dogs in *A Textbook for Teaching the Blind*. However, there is no evidence to suggest that his ideas made it any further than the printed page.

It was to be the First World War that gave real impetus to the movement, spearheaded by a German doctor who was determined to somehow ease the burden on the ever-growing number of soldiers returning from the front lines with their sight destroyed by poison gas. The story goes that his inspiration arrived one day in the early part of the war as he walked with a blind veteran through the gardens of a hospital. Stalling was called away to deal with an emergency and left the patient in the company of his dog, a German shepherd. On returning to the man sometime later, he observed that the dog was acting differently from normal: he was, it seemed to the doctor, looking out for the blind man.

Stalling set about investigating the practicalities of training dogs as reliable and safe guides, no doubt borrowing heavily from Klein. By August 1916, he was ready to open the world's first school for the training of guide dogs, which was based in Oldenburg. Within a few years, its success and reputation was such that there were a further nine branches throughout the country, providing those in need with some 600 fully trained animals per year.

It is a sad indictment of that sorry age that it didn't even come even close to satisfying demand, as the battlefields of Europe threw up more and more victims. Working in such difficult circumstances, standards were not always maintained and there began to be complaints that some of the dogs were not up to the job. By 1926, Stalling's network had outlived its usefulness and the decision was taken to close the schools down.

However, it had successfully proved that dogs could be trained to serve as a human's eyes and, fortunately, a new school had by then been established in Potsdam. Well equipped to fill the gap left by Stalling's enterprise, it soon won an international reputation. An American woman, Dorothy Harrison Eustis, was at the time living in Switzerland and training canines for various government authorities. She paid a visit to Potsdam and was so impressed by what she saw that she wrote an article for an American newspaper in 1927, which was in turn related to a blind man called Morris Frank. He made contact with Eustis, who subsequently trained a dog for him, leading directly to the establishment of the Seeing Eye dog-training programme in the US. Guide dogs came to the UK in 1930 and now play an important role in the lives of hundreds of thousands throughout the world.

The First Surgeon to Use General Anaesthetic: Seish Hanaoka

For the Western world, surgery became an infinitely more endurable prospect with the emergence of general anaesthetics in the 1840s. At the forefront of the movement, which ended millennia of appallingly inadequate methods of pain relief for those unfortunate enough to need an operation, was an American, Dr Crawford Williamson Long, who could safely knock out his patients with the use of sulphuric ether. Yet, unknown to him and his fellow pioneers, a Japanese surgeon by the name of Seishū Hanaoka had been operating with the use of general anaesthetics some 35 years earlier.

The reason for Hanaoka's lack of recognition in the West was the result of Japan's then policy of isolationism, an attempt to ward off the influence of European Christian missionaries that had the effect of cutting off the country in a way reminiscent of North Korea today. Hanaoka was born in a small town, Hirayama, in 1760, over 20 years after the government had expelled all Europeans from the country. The only exceptions were the Dutch, who continued to trade and were deemed just about acceptable as they largely kept their religion to themselves.

By the time Hanaoka had decided on a career in medicine in the 1780s, Japanese medicine had undergone something of a revolution based on the study of Dutch textbooks. Whereas Japanese students had previously learned anatomy from not entirely accurate drawings contained within ancient Chinese texts (dissection being then illegal in Japan), they now had the far more useful examples from modern Europe from which to learn. Hanaoka moved to Kyoto in 1782 to further his education and there took lessons in the Dutch school of surgery. When he returned to his hometown to take over his father's medical practice in 1785, he could call on a mixture of ancient Eastern and modern Western traditions.

With a particular desire to find a way of fighting the scourge of female breast cancer, he sought a means of carrying out operations to remove tumours without causing pain to the sufferer. While the Dutch offered little of value in terms of anaesthesia, there was a rather longer tradition in China, albeit of the local rather than general type. So he started to experiment with various traditional compositions of herbs in a bid to find something potent enough to render a subject fully unconscious for a decently long period without killing them altogether.

When he felt he might be nearing the right mix, he would test out his formulae on cats and dogs and then, if still encouraged by the results, on his willing wife. Tragically, she was to go blind as a direct result of her willingness to cooperate in her husband's exploits.

Eventually, after some 20 years, Hanaoka hit the jackpot with a potion he called *tsusensan*, the primary ingredients of which were angel's trumpet and monkshood (containing the active ingredients atropine and scopolamine, still used today). On 13 October 1804, he put a 60-year-old female patient, Kan Aiya, under the knife, having knocked her out with *tsusensan*. The woman was suffering from advanced breast cancer and, in desperation, had entrusted herself to the surgeon. He proceeded to successfully execute a mastectomy on the left breast and the woman lived a further six months before succumbing to the cancer that had already spread throughout her body before Hanaoka's intervention.

He went on to perform at least 150 further operations under general anaesthetic and trained more than 2,000 students in his methods. He died in 1835 and Japan did not open up to foreigners again until 1853, by which time the rest of the world had belatedly stumbled on general anaesthetics without ever being able to make use of Hanaoka's remarkable discoveries.

The First Person to Wear Dentures: Unidentified Mexican Man, circa 2500 bc

For most of human history, the use of dentures has been something of a hit-and-miss business. Things did not start to improve until the nineteenth century, with the marrying of high-quality porcelain teeth and vulcanite plates to keep them in place. Before that, you would have had to make do with ill-fitting human or animal teeth (there was a minor industry in excavating the teeth from the mouths of the young slain during the Napoleonic Wars) or artificial gnashers carved from bone or ivory. George Washington's famous set was actually made of hippopotamus ivory, rather than the wood of legend. During the reign of Elizabeth I, dentures were tied into place with silk string but were so unsatisfactory that the Virgin Queen actually chose to plug the gaps in her mouth with linen bungs when she was seen out in public.

Despite the absence of the necessary know-how to create wearable and good-looking dentures, our dental vanity has seemingly got the better of us for millennia.

In 2006, a team of archaeologists digging in the mountainous Michoacán state of southwest Mexico was led by native Purepecha Indians to a burial site beneath cliffs adorned with remarkable ancient artworks.

There they found the body of a man who had died some 4,500 years earlier. He had been aged somewhere between his late twenties and early thirties and stood a little over 1.5 metre (5 feet) tall. His corpse had been placed on a rock, with another rock put on top of him. Most extraordinary of all was the fact that his upper front teeth had been removed during his lifetime, cut right down to the gum to expose the pulp cavity. The assumption by the academics who viewed him was that they had most likely been extracted to make space for a set of dentures, possibly made from wolf or jaguar teeth. This would be the first set of false teeth that we know of.

The wearer of these strange fangs displayed signs of being well fed and unused to hard physical labour, suggesting that he was a figure of some standing in his community – perhaps a priest or shaman, giving rise to the possibility that his dentures served a ceremonial or ritualistic purpose. For instance, in other ancient Mexican traditions, including the Mayan, the Underworld was believed to be ruled by the big cat, so there may have been great symbolism attached to the wearing of jaguar teeth. However, others have argued the case that this early example of dental work was undertaken for purely cosmetic reasons. The likelihood is that the true motivation will never be known for sure.

It should also be noted that the man's cause of death was unclear but there were two significant abscesses in his mouth around the removed teeth, and so the possibility that he died of related blood poisoning is a real one. Yet the question remains as to whether we are any less scared of a visit to the dentist today ...

The First Computer Programmer: Ada Lovelace

Who would have thought that the daughter of the man so famously described as 'mad, bad and dangerous to know' would turn out to be the original computer geek?

Ada was born on 10 December 1815, the illegitimate daughter of Lord Byron and Annabella Milbanke. Her mother was not the first woman to be treated rather badly by the great poet, and so Ada was brought up estranged from her father until Byron's death when she was nine. Indeed, her mother was so averse to Ada's taking after him temperamentally and psychologically that she set about training her to be something entirely different. This included exposing her to the tutorage of some of the sharpest mathematical and scientific minds of the age. It was an area in which Ada turned out to be greatly gifted.

An attractive, lithe and charming girl, Ada spent a childhood blighted by ill health, which provided her with time to mull over mathematical conundrums. In 1833, she was first introduced to Charles Babbage, who would prove to be one of the most important influences on her life. She married William King in 1835 (he would later be made Earl of Lovelace) and lived in luxury on their Surrey estate, but her intellectual pursuits never faltered.

Shortly before his first meeting with Ada, Babbage had invented his 'Difference Engine', a machine capable of executing complex calculations automatically. It weighed in at 15 tons and was 2.4 metres (8 feet) high, the dimensions necessary for all the hardware required to do its work. Babbage did not see the machine through to completion before he started having grand new ideas for something slicker and better – his 'Analytical Engine', widely regarded as the world's earliest computer. The problem was, while he had no problems finding funding for his earlier project, the Analytical Engine was rather more complicated to explain and, besides, what guarantee was there that he would manage to take the project to fruition?

Thus it was that the Engine was destined to remain something that occupied only the theoretical realm. In 1842, he lectured in Italy on his ideas and among his audience was one Luigi Menabrea, who wrote a treatise on the subject. Babbage asked Ada, or 'The Enchantress of Numbers', as he called her, to translate the work into English. This she did, along with copious commentary notes of her own that tripled the length of Menabrea's original text.

In the process, she envisioned how Babbage's invention could evolve into something very similar to the modern computer. She understood the potential for an internal memory, the concept of artificial intelligence and even how the Engine might be used to produce electronic music. Her last set of notes, 'Section G', included detailed instructions on how the theoretical machine could be manipulated to calculate a sequence of Bernoulli numbers (a complicated sequence discovered by Swiss mathematician Jakob Bernoulli some 130 years earlier). Retrospectively, it has been recognised that this 'Section G' constitutes the world's first successful piece of computer programming – an achievement all the more remarkable for coming at a time when women and science were still widely regarded as an unhappy mix.

Alas, just as Ada's early years were tinged by ill health, so were her last. As Babbage struggled to realise his dreams, the relationship between the two seems to have drifted a little and Ada turned increasingly to drink and ill-advised dalliances. She died from cancer on 27 November 1852, leaving significant gambling debts and a collection of illicit love letters that her husband had burned. Long written out of history, a few monuments now exist to pay testament to her importance in the field of information technology, not least of which was a computer language especially created for use by the US Secretary of Defense that was named after her.

The First Fax-Machine Maker: Alexander Bain

The fax machine was a symbol of the 1980s, along with bricklike mobile phones and unfeasibly large shoulder pads. Yet it was a machine that had been a long time in the making, the earliest model having been created by Scotsman Alexander Bain way back in the mid-nineteenth century.

Bain was born in Caithness, Scotland, in 1811 and trained as a clockmaker. In 1837, he moved to London to ply his trade and there attended a series of lectures and demonstrations that fuelled his fascination with electricity. Eager to seek out new ways to harness its potential, he subsequently invented the world's first electric clock, which functioned using a pendulum regulated by an electromagnet.

With the advance of the electric age, the telegraph had also come into its own during the 1830s, allowing messages to be sent down cables in a way never previously imagined. Bain then came up with an invention he called the 'chemical telegraph', which essentially used the same electric signals as in a traditional telegraph but passed them through a specially developed paper coated in a mix of nitrate ammonia/prussiate of potash. The signal caused the evaporation of the solution to leave either a white Morse-code 'dot' or 'dash' on the page, greatly speeding up message transmission.

He next turned his mind to developing this creation with an eye to transmitting images as well as text. To do this, he plundered the technology in his electric clock, building a machine consisting of a pair of pendulums fitted with electric contacts and synchronised by electromagnets. The 'transmitting' pendulum swung over a copper plate on which a simple picture had been produced. Each time it made contact with the image, an electric pulse was generated and sent to the 'receiving' pendulum, which swung over a sheet of chemically coated paper, leaving a blue mark as required. With each swing, a one millimetre portion of the picture was scanned and copied. It may not have been pacy, nor was the copy image of great quality, but this was a huge technological leap. He formally patented his 'fax machine' on 27 May 1843, which, curiously, means that it predates the telephone by over three decades.

An Italian, Giovanni Caselli, took Bain's work on another stage, creating the 'pantelegraph', which formed the basis of the first commercial fax connection, opened between Paris and Lyon in 1865. Into the twentieth century, still more inventors evolved the system to make it a staple of the commercial world. But, for all its refinements, Bain's basic principle of using electricity to scan an image in one place and reproduce it in another remained the same. It was an idea that the world was still catching up with 140 years later.

As for Bain, he invented much else in his life, from railway signalling equipment to unspillable inkwells. However, an unfortunate bent for getting involved in lengthy patent disputes cost him both energy and his hard-won fortune. He died on 2 April 1877 at the Broomhill Home for Incurables in his native Scotland, having relied financially in his later years on an annuity secured by an influential patron.

The First Company to Produce a Wristwatch: Jaquet-Droz et Leschot

Pierre Jaquet-Droz was born in La Chaux-de-Fonds, Switzerland, on 28 July 1721. He would grow up to be one of the most revered clock- and watchmakers to have ever lived. Tucked away among the many achievements of his firm was the invention of the wristwatch in 1790.

Jaquet-Droz opened his first workshop in his hometown in 1738 and, having completed studies in mathematics, physics and theology, soon built a reputation for the quality of his wares. In the mid-1750s, he took on as his apprentice a young lad, Jean-Frédéric Leschot, who was to become not only a valued professional colleague but also an integral part of his family. A natural son, Henri-Louis, had also been born to Jaquet-Droz in 1752.

The step-up from respected craftsman to major European player came in 1758, when he travelled to Spain and sold several musical clocks to King Ferdinand VI. His fame was to become even greater in the 1760s and 1770s, when he created three incredible, humanlike automata (the Writer, the Musician and the Draughtsman), each made from several thousand components. These early robots went on a world tour, delighting the many rich and powerful who set eyes on them and today they remain the centrepiece of the Musée d'Art et d'Histoire in Neuchâtel.

By the 1780s, he had brought both Leschot and Henri-Louis into the management of his business, which now included workshops in London and Geneva. The company of Jaquet-Droz et Leschot was formed around 1784. At this juncture in the history of horology, watches were virtually all carried by gents, who kept them on chains and safely tucked in pockets. But about 1790, the Jaquet-Droz et Leschot workshop in Geneva included reference in its accounts book to 'a watch to be fixed to a bracelet'. An ornate diamond-encrusted piece specifically to be worn on a female wrist, this was very much jewellery rather than an item of great practical use.

Jaquet-Droz had an unerring knack for establishing working partnerships with the finest craftsmen available and keeping up with the latest technological developments, producing timepieces and novelty automata (chirruping birds in cages were another great favourite) that sold to wealthy buyers around the globe. Much of his work was heavily influenced by Chinese artistic traditions, as he sought to serve not only the Eastern market but also Europeans eager to sate their appetite for all things Oriental.

The trend for wearing such a novelty bracelet found great popularity among the ladies of the European upper classes but the arrival of the gents' equivalent was still a long way off. It would be virtually another hundred years before army commanders, eager to ensure that military manoeuvres were precisely synchronised, realised that a wristwatch was far more practical in the field than a cumbersome pocket watch.

Wilhelm I of Germany made the first significant purchase of men's wristwatches when he ordered some 2,000 from a rival Swiss manufacturer in 1879 for distribution among his armed forces. Some historians have suggested that the Second Boer War (1899–1902) was crucially influenced by the willingness of the British Army to make use of the wristwatch. Their widespread distribution to troops in the First World War led to an explosion in civilian demand in the 1920s, and the industry has never looked back. But it was Jaquet-Droz et Leschot who set the ball rolling by creating and filling the market for dainty ladies' wristwatches back in the late eighteenth century.

The First Email Sender: Ray Tomlinson

Was there *really* a time before emails? An age when we physically had to get words on to paper, a process involved enough that we had time to consider coolly whether it was wise to send the message in the first place? Well, yes, there was such an age and, remarkably, it wasn't that long ago!

Ray Tomlinson was born in New York in 1941. Having gained a master's degree from the Massachusetts Institute of Technology in 1967, he began working for Bolt, Beranek and Newman, a cutting-edge information-technology company based in Cambridge, Massachusetts. There he found himself deployed on projects concerned with the ARPANET Network Control Protocol, a US Department of Defense creation that proved to be the forerunner of the Internet that we have today.

Nascent email technology had been developed by another MIT alumnus, Fernando Corbato, in 1965, when he came up with a system that allowed electronic messages to be sent between users sharing the same computer. ARPANET had a similar system of its own called SNDMSG. Tomlinson was developing a file-transfer program, CYPNET, when he wrote a 200-line piece of software incorporating code from both technologies to allow messages to be sent from one computer to another entirely.

Tomlinson gave his new program its first test run in the latter part of 1971, sending messages between computers a few yards from each other in the same room. He endearingly covered the ground between them by wheelie chair, eager to see if his words had been sent and received correctly. Unfortunately, as with so many emails sent today, the text of Tomlinson's inaugural missive was, by his own admission, highly forgettable. His best guess was that he probably typed 'QUERTYUIOP' (the letters on the top line of a keyboard), 'TESTING 1-2-3' or something equally unworthy of a great moment in history.

The first message of note was to other members of his work team to alert them to his success. As he would later comment, 'The first use of network email announced its own existence.' His colleague, Jerry Burchfiel, reputedly greeted the arrival of email with the (tongue-in-cheek) advice, 'Don't tell anyone! This isn't what we're supposed to be working on.'

Tomlinson was also responsible for making the '@' symbol universally recognised when he chose it to be used in email addresses to indicate which host network the user is 'at'. He was using a Model 33 Teletype keyboard at the time and, from a selection of just 12 punctuation characters, he plumped for '@' on account of its being the only preposition available to him. His own address was 'tomlinson@bbn-tenexa', BBN being his employer and Tenex the operating system he was using.

Tomlinson knew he had come up with what he described as 'a neat idea', but just how influential his work would become was surely beyond the limits of even his imagination.

The First Safe-Sex Advocate: Gabriele Falloppio

The condom, or variants thereof, has been used by civilisations throughout the world for thousands of years, made from materials as disparate as animal intestines, leather, paper and tortoiseshell (the last, used in Japan, particularly bringing a tear to the eye!). But, crucially, the condom was always used as a contraceptive, not as a barrier against disease, apart from a short spell in the

Roman era when there was a suggestion that it might help fend off Mount Vesuvius' Rash (as venereal diseases were generically named) among the Empire's young soldiers.

Europe was to witness a steep rise in sexually transmitted infections from the fifteenth to the seventeenth centuries, with outbreaks of syphilis and assorted other diseases contracted by lusty sailors on their adventures in the New World. The stage was set for Gabriele Falloppio (sometime known as Fallopius), born in Modina in 1523 into a down-at-heel noble family. He initially went into the Church, becoming canon of Modena Cathedral in 1542, before turning to medicine. He undertook his studies at the medical school in Ferrara, taking a post as professor of anatomy there in 1548. The following year, he joined the faculty at the prestigious University of Pisa, and in 1551 Cosimo I, Duke of Tuscany, summoned him to the University of Padua.

Today, Falloppio is best known as the man who donated his name to the tube connecting the ovary to the uterus. However, in his own lifetime he was much celebrated for the work he carried out on the anatomy of the ears, eyes and nose. He was also a prodigious author and in 1564 wrote a treatise (not published during his lifetime) on syphilis. It was entitled *De Morbo Gallico*, the ailment then being known as the French disease (except in France, where it was known as the Italian disease!). In this work, he described how a linen sheath, marinated in a herbal potion, could be fitted over the tip of the penis and under the foreskin to stave off the illness. Crucially, this was the first time that a medical practitioner had outlined the use of condoms as a means of maintaining sexual health as opposed to preventing pregnancy.

With a dramatic flourish, his design incorporated a pink ribbon to keep what must have been the rather uncomfortable article in place. Falloppio claimed to have conducted a clinical trial of the device involving 1,100 males, none of whom contracted syphilis. Success indeed. It fell to his near contemporary at Padua, Hercules Saxonia (1551–1606), to develop the concept into a larger sheath to be worn over the whole male member.

Falloppio died in Padua on 9 October 1562 of suspected tuberculosis, not yet 40 but considered one of the great anatomists of the age. The *Catholic Encyclopedia* of 1913 was glowing, if predictably oblique, in its praise of *De Morbo Gallico*: 'His treatise on syphilis is wonderful in anticipation of what is sometimes thought most modern in this subject.'

'I've been thinking long and hard on how to improve on the hobby horse, McMillan... and I suspect the answer is Lycra shorts.'

CHAPTER FIVE

Transport

The First Public Railway: The Surrey Iron Railway

A year before George Stephenson successfully tested his legendary steam locomotive, the Rocket, and, a full 27 years before the opening of the world's first passenger steam railway, the Liverpool & Manchester, there was a revolution under way in a quiet corner of what is now south London.

The Surrey Iron Railway (SIR) most certainly belonged to a different age: it was built to allow horse-drawn wagons to cart tons of industrial produce along iron rails. Indeed, in the planning stages it was referred to as a 'plateway' and not a railway at all. However, by the time it opened in 1803, it was the first railway in the world to market itself as such. Far more importantly, it proved to the many sceptics the viability of laying a rail network and of attracting paying customers to make use of it. As such, it was a significant step on the journey towards the rail networks that stretch around the world today.

At the end of the eighteenth century, the part of Surrey to be catered for by the SIR was home to many and varied industries producing goods in countless mills and factories. Industrial leaders were adamant that they had to be able to transport their output the nine miles from Croydon to Wandsworth. The initial thinking was that this could best be achieved by building a canal link, only for the plans to falter when the ground was found to be unsuitable for such a feat of engineering. So attention turned to the idea of a horse-drawn railway, a scheme that won parliamentary support in 1801.

William Jessop was the engineer chosen to see the project through, something he achieved at a cost of £7,000 generated from the railway's shareholders, who were by and large the owners of the factories and mills along its route. A double track was laid, allowing transport to go in both directions. The rails were made of cast iron and laid some 127 centimetres (4 feet 2 inches) apart (making it a narrow-gauge line). The SIR was officially opened on 26 July 1803 and farmers, traders and industrialists immediately took advantage of it, paying tolls of between 1d (one old penny) and 3d per ton of goods carried per mile. Horses and donkeys were used to pull wagon trains of three or four carriages at a time, reaching speeds of 4 miles per hour.

Within a couple of years, extensions to Merstham, Godstone, Hackbridge and Mitcham were added and for a while there was an ambitious plan to extend the railway all the way down to Portsmouth. However, a lack of finance ensured that this grand scheme never got off the ground. In 1807, the SIR was followed by the world's first fare-charging passenger railway, which opened in Wales and served Swansea and the Mumbles.

In 1823, an approach was made to George Stephenson about the possibility of providing the SIR with steam locomotives but, unfortunately, the track was not robust enough to endure the necessary weights. Having done so much to prove the workability of the railways, the Surrey Iron Railway was soon rendered obsolete in the age of steam and was closed for good in 1846.

The First Automobile Fatality: Bridget Driscoll

Poor Mrs Driscoll has the dubious honour of being the first recorded person to die in a car accident. Sadly, she did not even have the pleasure of racing around in one of the new machines when tragedy struck on 17 August 1896.

It was perhaps a blessing that it took 11 years from Karl Benz's demonstration of the first commercial motor car for the first person to lose their life. On the morning in question, Bridget, a 44-year-old mother of two, was enjoying a trip to the Crystal Palace in London to watch a dance demonstration with her teenage daughter and her daughter's friend.

As she was crossing the grounds, a 20-year-old man from Upper Norwood called Arthur Edsall was giving test drives on behalf of the Anglo-French Motor Company. A recently established Birmingham-based company, Anglo-French manufactured Roger-Benz cars with some minor alterations for the UK market. In an era when driving tests simply did not exist, the company does not seem to have been overly concerned by the fact that Edsall had only three weeks' driving experience under his belt.

At the time of the accident, he was demonstrating the vehicle to a Miss Alice Standing. It has been suggested that, like many others who followed him, Edsall was a young man in a machine intent on wowing a fair maiden. At the subsequent inquest, Miss Standing intimated that Edsall may have adjusted the engine in an early attempt at 'souping up'. An engineer, though, reported that there was no evidence of such tampering. Nonetheless, an eyewitness claimed that the car had been going at 'a reckless pace; in fact, like a fire engine'. It was out 4mph, which was certainly To give some context, that same ecame the first man convicted of regarded the 2mph limit in a built-

rtling towards her, it seems that Mrs n to the spot. She was knocked to the her skull in the process, and was dead s. The coroner's inquest was held in after six hours of deliberation, a verdict of ath' was returned. Edsall escaped without The coroner, one Percival Morrison, rather ly stated his desire that 'such a thing would en again'.

irst Traffic Lights: Parliament Square, London

pitiful truism that road traffic breeds road hogs. h the rapid increase in vehicle numbers from the d-Victorian era right up to the present day, authorities have needed to be ever more ingenious in devising ways to make the highways safe. There has been perhaps no greater weapon in the war than traffic lights, a staple in virtually every country of the world. They were introduced to London in 1868, but their initial stay was rather short-lived.

On 9 December of that year, a set was installed at the

junction of Great George Street and Bridge
stone's throw from Westminster Bridge. They w
brainchild of John Peake (J. P.) Knight, a
railwayman who had been born in Nottingham in
In 1866, as a superintendent of the South-E
Railway, he gave evidence before a House of Com
committee that found in favour of introducing
signals to regulate metropolitan traffic.

Knight, charged with coming up with a suit
design, opted for a pillar some 7.3 metres (24 feet) h
with semaphore arms. When the arms were set at
degrees to the pillar it meant 'stop', and at 45 degr
'caution'. Essentially, the signals replicated what a traf
policeman would otherwise do with his arms. In t
dark of night, additional red and green lights aide
identification. The set of signals was manufactured by
Saxby and Farmer, long-established manufacturers of
railway signals. They produced a fine-looking structure,
the ornate iron pillar weighing in at some 5 tons and
painted green 'relieved with gilding'.

However, tragedy was to strike on 2 January 1869, a
mere three weeks or so after the lights went up. A leaky
gas valve caused one of the lights to explode, severely
burning the face of the police officer who was operating
it. The traffic-light experiment was brought to a
premature end and the lights removed. They were not to

return to the streets of London for another 60 years. As for Knight, he finished his career as general manager of the Brighton Railway Company and died on 23 July 1886 after suffering an apoplectic fit.

Incidentally, at the turn of the third millennium, the tiny Himalayan state of Bhutan made a bid to catch up with the rest of the world by erecting its first set of traffic lights in the capital, Thimphu. In a nation where it is official policy to pursue 'gross domestic happiness', their stay was only a little longer than those in Parliament Square, as it was decided that they were an eyesore and they were promptly torn down.

The First Steamship to Cross the Atlantic:
SS Savannah

The Atlantic Ocean has seen many famous crossings, from Christopher Columbus to the *Titanic*, but one of the lesser known was symbolically among the most important. In 1819, the SS *Savannah* made the journey from New York to Liverpool, going at least part of the way under steam. As such, the voyage was an important staging post in ushering out the age of the sail ships and welcoming in the age of modern maritime travel.

Savannah was built by the shipyard of Fickett & Crocker in New York in 1818 and owned by Scarborough & Isaacs, a Georgian shipping firm. In respect of her owners' home state, she was given the name of its famous port city. Moses Rogers was appointed the ship's captain and it was he who carried the dream of fitting out this traditional sail ship (about 30 metres/100 feet long and 320 metric tons) with a steam engine and paddle to turn her into the first transatlantic passenger steamer. Fitted with a 90hp engine and a wheel some 4.8 metres (about 16 feet) across, she had the facility to carry 75 metric tons of coal and 25 tons of wood fuel.

Decked out with sleeping berths for 32 people, *Savannah* was celebrated for her spaciousness and luxurious feel. However, that counted for little when Moses set about finding a crew and passengers to join him on the historic maiden voyage. Understandably, there was widespread resistance to signing up as guinea pigs on such an experimental trip, despite *Savannah*'s having already hosted then president James Monroe on a short domestic route.

The date of 22 May 1819 was selected for the start of the trip, the ship running with a skeleton staff, no passengers and barely any freight. The omens were not good when one of the crew fell from a gangplank and drowned just two days before the trip was due to begin. Nonetheless, the voyage went exceedingly smoothly, barring a couple of engagements with other vessels convinced that the smoke produced by the boiler was a sign that the ship was on fire.

Having been at sea for 29 days, she made her way into the port of Liverpool on 20 June 1819 to be greeted by thousands of well-wishers. Of those 29 days, she was under steam for somewhat less than four. From Liverpool, she went first to Stockholm, where King Charles XIV made an offer to buy her, and then on to Russia to see Tsar Alexander II. The Homewood leg of the trip, from Norway to Georgia, was done entirely under sail and took around 40 days.

In 1829, Scarborough & Isaacs came off badly after a fire raged through the city of Savannah and they were forced to sell the ship (without its engine). SS *Savannah* subsequently served as a pleasure cruiser on a route between Georgia and New York. In November 1821, she ran aground on Long Island, an event that ended her days as an active vessel. However, in her prime she had proved that a steam vessel was fit for even the most arduous journeys on the ocean wave and paved the way for the great ships of the years following the Industrial Revolution.

The First Manned Cross-Channel Flight: Blanchard & Jeffries

Ever since Icarus came to his sticky end, man has been fascinated by how he might conquer the skies. But it was not until 1783 and the emergence of the Montgolfier brothers' successful hot-air balloon that he could claim that flying among the clouds was anything more than pie in the sky.

The success of the Montgolfiers spurred on Jean-Pierre Blanchard, who was born in Normandy in 1753 with a bent for engineering and the arrogance necessary to so many great pioneers. Having messed about with a winged bicycle contraption, Blanchard spent the spring and summer of 1783 quietly experimenting with hydrogen balloons, making several successful flights, including one from Rouen to Bordeaux. The problem was that every Tom, Dick and Henri was getting into the balloon business in France, so Blanchard decided to relocate to London, where he could more easily guarantee funding.

Among his patrons was a Bostonian doctor called John Jeffries and the two men took their first joint flight at the end of November 1784. Together they hit upon a plan to be the first to fly across the Channel, a challenge that would not only further the cause of ballooning but would also undoubtedly secure them personal fame.

However, for Blanchard, the doctor was no more than an open wallet and, while happy to take his money, he was exceedingly unwilling to share in any glory. Nonetheless, the two men and a suitable balloon were in place to make the attempt on 7 January 1785, when the story descends into farce. Blanchard locked himself away in Dover Castle and refused to communicate with Jeffries until strong-armed by some sailors Jeffries had employed. Blanchard then claimed that the balloon, which carried only about 13 kilos (30 pounds) of ballast, was not capable of transporting two men, and suggested he should perhaps go alone. When Jeffries protested, Blanchard set out to prove that the balloon could not cope with their combined weight, shortly before Jeffries revealed that his companion had weighed himself down by tying a lead-lined belt round his middle. In the end, Blanchard agreed that Jeffries could go, but on condition that the doctor throw himself overboard should the necessity arise.

They eventually took off at a few minutes past one o'clock in the afternoon. In almost perfect conditions, a crowd of several hundred waved them off until they were out of view of the cliffs of Dover. As it happened, the balloon did indeed fail to achieve the necessary altitude and much of the flight was spent precariously skimming the waves. So they set about unburdening the vehicle, ridding themselves of several wholly unnecessary devices that Blanchard had insisted on, including oars, a non-functioning propeller and all manner of steering equipment.

With the French coast still several miles away and virtually everything that could be thrown out now gone, the balloon remained dangerously low. At that point, the two men started disrobing, flinging coats, shirts and eventually trousers overboard. They even resorted to attempting to evacuate their own bodies of any extraneous weight, with Jeffries reporting how they 'did their utmost to relieve themselves as much as possible'!

Wearing cork lifejackets and preparing to entrust their fates to the sea, they suddenly found themselves propelled by the wind, and were able to finish the journey, landing in a tree a few miles outside Calais a little over two hours after take-off. They were picked up by a rescue party, who must have wondered at the two be-panted gents in their basket.

In the aftermath, both men were much fêted, and Blanchard was honoured by Louis XVI and awarded a significant pension. He set up a ballooning school in London and travelled the continent wowing crowds with his exploits. When the French Revolution began in 1789, he briefly found himself in the custody of the Austrians before fleeing to America, where in 1792 he made the first untethered flight that nation had ever seen. His last flight came in Holland in 1808, during which he had a heart attack and crash-landed. Having never recovered fully, he died in Paris on 7 March 1809.

The First Parachutist: André-Jacques Garnerin

It takes a particular sort of personality to be the first to volunteer to throw yourself out of a balloon high among the clouds and bet your survival on an untested silk canopy. The owner of just such a character was a keen French balloonist by the name of André-Jacques Garnerin.

Born in Paris on 31 January 1769, Garnerin had a passion for physics and a fascination with aviation. There were a couple of developments during his teens that may well have sparked a particular interest in parachutes. First, Louis-Sébastien Lenormand developed a prototype parachute cobbled together from a couple of umbrellas and used it to leap to safety from a tree. Then, in 1885, Jean-Pierre Blanchard (*see previous entry*) came up with a parachute attached to a basket, which he tested from an air balloon. Or, strictly speaking, he volunteered a small kitten to carry out the test, which, thankfully, survived the ordeal.

Garnerin had already started work on his own canopies when he was sent off to serve in Napoleon's army. He was quickly captured by the British, who gave him over to the Austrian authorities, who, in turn, imprisoned him in Budapest. While there, he apparently entertained notions that he might somehow parachute himself to freedom, though he never got as far as making an attempt.

He was eventually liberated by more traditional means (the Austrians freed him) and he returned to Paris to renew his work on a workable canopy. He was ready to make his inaugural test jump on 22 October 1797 at the Parc Monceau in Paris. Having ascended in a hydrogen balloon to a height of about 915 metres (3,000 feet), he cut the balloon free and opened his 7-metre-wide (23-foot) semi-rigid canopy, which looked for all the world like a giant umbrella. He was contained within a basket beneath it.

The breeze caught hold of the canopy and the crowds below feared for their intrepid hero, but, despite a slightly ragged descent, he reached the ground unhurt save for a sprained ankle sustained on impact. He made many more demonstration jumps, as well as balloon ascents, over the years, entertaining the crowds in Paris at the Tivoli Gardens and bringing his spectacle to London in 1802. Four years earlier, his wife Jeanne-Genevieve had become the first woman parachutist.

Daredevilry seems to have been in the Garnerin genes, for the couple were eventually joined in their exploits by their niece, Elisabeth, who made her first jump in 1815. She became the world's first professional parachutist, making 39 jumps in a career that brought her fame across Europe. Alas, André-Jacques was destined for a sad and early end when in 1823 he was struck across the head by a heavy beam while in the process of preparing a balloon for flight.

The First Ambulance Service: Dominique-Jean Larrey's Flying Ambulance

The use of a vehicle to get first aid to an injured party and then to take the patient on to a suitable centre for more thorough medical attention was born amid the gore and slaughter of the Napoleonic battlefields.

'Ambulances' were first recorded in the late fifteenth century during the reign of the Spanish Queen Isabella. However, these bore little resemblance to what we think of as ambulances today. Rather, they were mobile field hospitals that followed the army round and could pick up and treat casualties once an engagement was over. This system was little changed by the time Dominique-Jean Larrey was appointed surgeon-major of Napoleon's Army of the Rhine in 1792.

Larrey had been born in the small Pyrenean village of Beaudean in 1766. He started his medical training when just 14 years old under the tutelage of his famed physician uncle, Alexis Larrey. When he was 21, he moved to Toulouse to continue his studies and was then engaged as a ship's doctor. Later, he found his way to Paris, where he was expected to treat appalling injuries as the French Revolution raged.

During the Rhine campaign of 1792, he was struck by the delay in treatment that casualties had to endure under the old-style 'ambulance' system. He considered how many young men had lost their lives as a result of delays (particularly in executing necessary amputations), while at the same time he was able to admire the efficiency of the wheeled French artillery in getting around the place. Thus, he came to propose to his military seniors 'the plan of an ambulance, calculated to follow the advanced guard in the same manner as the flying artillery'. This, he suggested, should be called the flying ambulance.

The idea was well received and Larrey researched the practicalities, deciding in the end on a system of horse-drawn carriages. It was given a first run-out during a skirmish close to the city of Limbourg (in modern Belgium) and was considered a resounding success. Larrey was thus charged with rolling out the programme to the French armies in other regions, although this was something he was unable to do until 1797 as a result of other commitments. In that year, he went to Italy and introduced his ambulances, consisting of a mixture of light and heavy carriages, each crewed by a seven-man team. The carriages were equipped with the facilities to dispense emergency treatment on the battlefield before moving the patients to a safer place, and there were windows to provide ventilation. Drawn by a pair of horses, each ambulance had either two or four wheels (depending on the terrain) and could transport two to four patients at a time.

He also introduced a revolutionary system of triage that prioritised patients on the basis of their need rather than by rank or nationality. The fame of Larrey spread not only among his own side but to the enemy as well. Few men were held in more esteem and it is said that, at the Battle of Waterloo in 1815, the Duke of Wellington ordered his troops to cease firing so that Larrey's ambulances could round up the injured.

Napoleon himself recognised Larrey as a masterful medic as well as a brilliant organiser, referring to him as 'the worthiest man I ever met' and making him a baron in 1809. After Waterloo, Larrey was captured by Prussian troops and sentenced to death but the punishment was commuted when his identity was established and he was returned under guard to France, where he lived out the rest of his life until 1842.

The First Pedal Cyclist: Kirkpatrick Macmillan

The earliest bicycles started appearing in the late eighteenth century, but they required nerves of steel and a hide of leather to risk a ride. Not the least of their problems was that they had no pedals, leaving the rider's feet inconveniently dragging along the ground. At least, that was the case until an unprepossessing Scottish blacksmith by the name of Kirkpatrick Macmillan appeared on the scene.

Born in 1812 in the small parish of Kier in Dumfriesshire, Macmillan started his working life when still a small boy, helping out at his father's forge and on various local farms. By the time he was in his early twenties, he was apprenticed to the blacksmith of the Duke of Buccleuch and it was around this time that he saw a man riding a most uncomfortable, pedal-less 'hobby-horse' (a primitive cycle of the sort popularised by the Comte Mede de Sivrac in the 1790s).

Macmillan decided he would have one himself and set about constructing a model along his own designs. When he had finished the build and had taught himself the intricacies of riding it, he was struck by how much simpler it would be if it could be propelled by pedals operated by feet kept a safe distance from the earth. He took himself off to his old dad's forge and made the necessary adjustments, emerging sometime in the middle of 1839 with the world's first pedal bike, weighing in at an aerodynamically challenging half-a-hundredweight.

It consisted of a wooden frame and iron-rimmed wooden wheels, the front one about 0.8 metre (2½ feet) in diameter and the back one a little over a metre (3½ feet). Macmillan was to become a regular sight on the roads around Dumfries in the months and years that followed, and won particular fame for what must have been a somewhat bone-shaking 68-mile journey to his brother in Glasgow. That jaunt took him a little over two days.

Alas, with improved vehicle efficiency and higher speeds came an increased risk of accidents. Around the time Macmillan made his trip to Glasgow, one of the city's newspapers reported a collision involving an unnamed 'man from Dumfries-shire' riding a cycle of 'ingenious design' and a small girl who had run across his path. The cyclist, fined five shillings (25p) for the incident, was identified as Macmillan himself by one of his descendants at the end of the nineteenth century.

While Macmillan doubtless loved his creation, he lacked a commercial eye and failed to register any kind of patent. Within a short while, others were making their own versions of the bicycle, notably Gavin Dalzell of Lesmahagow, who sold models for the significant sum of £6 or £7. Indeed, so successful was Dalzell that for several decades he, rather than Macmillan, received the credit as the inventor of the bicycle – a tale he was presumably happy to have peddled.

'The idea's bound to catch on once I've sorted
out a simpler name.'

CHAPTER SIX

The Commercial World

The First Supermarket Magnate: Michael Cullen

Michael J. Cullen, born the son of Irish immigrants in Newark, New Jersey, in 1884, had garnered significant experience in the retail sector before opening the world's first supermarket, called King Kullen, on 4 August 1930 in a former garage in the Jamaica section of Queens, New York, measuring about 557 square metres (6,000 square feet). Never a man to undersell himself, he offered his customers the 'low prices of the house of the promised land'.

In 1902, Cullen had joined the Great Atlantic & Pacific Tea Company, where he stayed for 17 years before moving on to Kroger Stores. Cullen's wife, Nan, would later recall that her husband first scoped out his plan for a supermarket in 1913, but the wheels did not get into motion until several years later.

In 1929, he wrote to Kroger's company president, William Albers, outlining his scheme and suggesting the company open five test stores, to be called Cullen Stores, throughout the country. His economic master plan involved selling some 300 items at cost price (to entice the customers in), 200 others at 5 per cent above cost, 300 more at 15 per cent above cost and another 300 at 20 per cent above cost. Albers would never respond to the letter and the following year Cullen took the brave decision to go it alone.

His spiritual forefather could be said to be one Clarence Saunders, who had opened the first self-service grocery store in 1916 in Memphis, Tennessee. He called his shop Piggly Wiggly (a brand name still in use to this day) and patented his idea in 1917, achieving massive commercial success before some unwise dabbling in the stock market in the 1920s forced him to sell his stake in the company he had founded.

Cullen ran with the idea of the self-service store, which at a stroke slashed store operating costs and gave consumers a sense of freedom of choice that they had previously lacked. But he went much further than any of his predecessors. His huge store was departmentalised for ease of use, prices were often massively discounted, everything was sold in volume (an unheard of 1,000 different lines were on offer from the outset) and customers could even take advantage of free parking. While none of these ideas came uniquely from Cullen, he was the first to put them all together.

The unusual store name came about as the result of a drawing by his son, Bobby, which depicted a man atop a globe whom Bobby labelled 'King Kullen'. While the shop's décor may not have been anywhere near palatial, people loved it and flocked through the doors. On at least one occasion, the police had to be called to keep order. By 1936, Cullen had opened 17 branches and was planning many more franchises nationwide.

The company was by then turning over $6 million per year (nearer $75 million in today's value). The future looked truly rosy until Cullen suffered complications after an appendicitis operation and died in 1936, aged just 52. In the four years following the opening of his flagship store, 1,200 further supermarkets had sprung up across America and the number has only risen ever since. A fitting legacy for the self-proclaimed 'World's Greatest Price Wrecker'.

The First Credit Card Holder: Frank McNamara

The first prophetic mention of a credit card came in a highly influential nineteenth-century American novel called *Looking Backward: 2000–1887*. Published in 1888 and written by Edward Bellamy, the book details the life of Julian West, a character who emerges from a 113-year coma at the turn of the third millennium. Among the many changes that have overcome American society is the introduction of credit cards, a creation of Bellamy's mind over 60 years before the real thing came into being.

It is said that in the autumn of 1949 McNamara was having lunch with a business associate at a favourite eatery in New York called Major's Cabin Grill. When the bill came, McNamara went to get his wallet, only to have one of those moments of excruciating embarrassment as he realised he had left it in another suit. Fortunately, he was able to make a call to his wife who came to the rescue, but at that moment Frank vowed never to be in that situation again.

The incident played on his mind for several weeks and he eventually broached the subject with his lawyer, Frank Schneider. McNamara had an idea for a 'club' whereby its members could eat at specific restaurants, sign for their meals on the spot and then pay up within a specified time period. The two men decided to found a company to implement this innovation, calling on Matty Simons to join as a partner. Alfred Bloomingdale (of the famous department-store family) would eventually buy out McNamara's share of the business.

By February 1950, the Diners Club was ready to go into operation, with some 200 cardholders personally invited by the company having joined up for a three-dollar fee. Unlike with most of our modern cards, any outstanding balance was to be paid by the end of each calendar month. The cardholder incurred no interest but companies who accepted it as payment paid a 7 per cent transaction fee to Diners Club.

To give the new card a proper launch, McNamara arranged a lunch for a collection of friends and colleagues back at Major's Cabin Grill. After they had sated their appetites and the bill arrived, Frank pulled out the small cardboard card, which was inscribed with the names of the 14 restaurants who had agreed to participate in the scheme. This meal became affectionately known as 'the First Supper'.

The card was an instant hit, so much so that the company had to make three rapid changes of office within its Empire State Building base to accommodate an expanding workforce. Within a year the Diners Club boasted 20,000 members and within two years there were franchises in Canada, Cuba and France. Such success naturally saw a rush of imitators with schemes gradually extending so that cards were accepted in ever greater numbers of locations, offering more credit over longer periods of time. American Express launched in 1958 and a year later the Bank of America launched a programme that evolved into the VISA card. By 1980, Diners Club itself was accepted in 450,000 locations and numbered 4.2 million members. Ten years later, McNamara was named by *Life* magazine as one of the hundred most influential Americans of the century. The age of the credit card, for better or worse, was upon us.

The First Factory Owner: Matthew Boulton

The idea of what constitutes a factory is a fluid one and thus convincing cases have been made for a number of sites as the first. There are those who have argued the case of the government-owned Venetian Arsenal, a sprawling area in which was concentrated the labour and capital to build and fit out armoured ships. Having first started production in the early years of the twelfth century, by the turn of the sixteenth, it was said to have housed a workforce of more than 15,000 and could churn out a completed vessel once a day.

Others point to the silk mill of John Lombe, which was built in Derby in 1721, after John's brother, Thomas, had smuggled designs of cutting-edge machinery from Italy. Designed by the famed engineer

George Sorocold, it had a great many features that we associate with the factory system. These included a single distinct owner, machinery running from a single power source (a waterwheel), a multistorey complex of buildings with different areas designed for specific stages of the process, administrative offices and warehousing facilities and a large workforce (up to 300 people).

However, it is the Soho Manufactory of Matthew Boulton, built close to Birmingham in the Midlands of England in 1761, that can best claim to be the first factory. It was highly mechanised, and its sizeable labour force was able to see through manufactures from raw material to complex finished products on a single purpose-built site.

Boulton was born in 1728 in Birmingham. His father ran a company producing small metal goods. Matthew took over the business while still a young man and developed it into one of Europe's most thriving, dealing in buttons and belt buckles, children's toys and highly fashionable ormolu wares. By 1761, he was a prosperous man and took the decision to rent several acres of land at Handsworth, including a mill and a large house, to which Boulton and his family moved in 1766. By then, he had already built his Manufactory along the designs of the architect William Wyatt.

Regarded as a wonder of the age, it consisted of a huge warehouse building, premises for various administrative staff, several metalworking workshops and accommodation for the workers. Boulton and his then business partner, John Fothergill, spent some £20,000 on the complex (getting on for £3 million in today's money).

The Manufactory really came into its own after Boulton met James Watt, the legendary Scottish pioneer of the steam engine. The two men joined forces in the mid-1770s and Boulton's premises became the centre of the production and exports of Watt's engines, which kept Britain's industrial heart pumping for years. 'I sell here, sir,' Boulton once remarked, 'what all the world desires to have – Power.'

Boulton eventually built the entirely separate Soho Foundry for the construction of engines. In later years, he also won the right to make coins for the Royal Mint, something his Soho Mint did to standards of excellence never previously known. In addition, Boulton was a prominent member of the Lunar Society, a collection of thinkers and doers who helped propel the Industrial Revolution, and they were often to meet in the luxurious surroundings of Soho House.

He died in 1809 at the age of 80, one of the leading lights of Britain's Industrial Revolution. If he was to have learned anything, it was that time could not stand in the way of industrial progress. So he may not have been too surprised when the great monument to his vision was torn down during the 1860s.

The First Vending Machine: Holy Water Dispenser, Egypt

Visitors to London in the early 1880s were able to wonder at a fantastic new device – a coin-operated postcard-vending machine. Americans, meanwhile, had to wait until the end of the decade before they got their own such machine, which sold chewing gum rather than postcards. It must have seemed like a brave new step in a rapidly commercialising world. The truth, though, was that the late-nineteenth-century vending machine was a re-creation of a device created some 1,800 years earlier to service the temples of ancient Egypt.

It was designed by Heron of Alexandria, a man of enormous importance to the development of mathematics and engineering but whose own life is something of a mystery. It is likely that he was born around AD 10 in Alexandria in Egypt. In common with many of the great thinkers of the ancient world, he wrote vast numbers of works on a disparate range of subjects. These included theses on surveying instruments, an automaton theatre, weapons and war machines, architecture and all sorts of steam-, air- and water-powered devices.

These latter machines were detailed in his two-volume *Pneumatica*, which provided designs for puppets, toys and musical instruments. It also laid out guidelines for a coin-operated machine. A coin was deposited through a slot in the top of the box and fell into a pan that, when weighed down, operated a lever. When the lever rose, it opened a valve that allowed water to flow out into a receptacle. When the lever had tilted far enough that the coin fell out of the pan, a counterweight returned it to its original position, closing off the valve and ceasing the flow of water.

Such a piece of engineering ingenuity was just what the religious houses of the highly devout Egyptian civilisation were crying out for. At the time there was a real problem with patrons helping themselves to far more holy water than they had paid for. Now here was a way of strictly rationing the supply while ensuring the books balanced, as punters had no choice but to pay up their five drachms (a standard Egyptian coin) per divine 'splash'. Quite why the technology fell into disuse for so many centuries afterwards is far from clear.

The First Launderette Owner: J. F. Cantrell

Beloved of students and jeans advertisers alike, the launderette is a classic example of a fine business idea borne out of difficult economic times. Known variously as Laundromats or Washeterias, the launderette first found a home in America's Deep South during the Great Depression, at a moment in history when vast numbers of women beheld the tantalising prospect of liberation from the mangle and posser (a tool of old used for 'possing' or mixing laundry while hand-washing it), but lacked the available cash to take advantage.

There can be no doubt that the invention of the automatic washing machine was one that offered far greater potential benefits to the female of the species than the male. From the earliest times, it had fallen largely to women to ensure that clothes and household fabrics were clean, a job that took up an inordinate proportion of the working week when everything had to be washed by hand.

The Hurley Machine Company of Chicago was the first to develop and sell an electric-powered washing machine when, in 1908, it brought out the impressively named Thor model. However, it was not cheap and much of America was still to be connected up to the national grid. Sales were slow and it was only by the late 1920s that they were getting anywhere near the million mark. Then the Wall Street Crash hit in 1929, prompting a collapse in the global economy that knocks our own depression of the noughties into a cocked hat. No longer was there disposable cash floating about for such utter luxuries as a washing machine. With it went the hope of imminent female emancipation from the drudgery of laundry.

But in testing circumstances great visionaries can emerge, and one such happened to be resident in Fort Worth, Texas. A gent by the name of J. F. Cantrell realised that, if he could somehow make the technology available to the public for a small hourly fee, he might expect to make himself a pretty dollar or two. So he bought four machines and installed them into individual cubicles all under one roof. Water and electricity came courtesy of the proprietor but customers were obliged to provide their own soap (and were sternly warned about clogging the machines with oversized quilts).

Cantrell decided to call his business the Washeteria, and its doors opened for the first time on 18 April 1934. It was an instant hit and Cantrell, of course, cleaned up.

The First Man to Use a Cash Machine: Reg Varney
The cashpoint, or automated teller machine (ATM), was invented by John Shepherd-Barron, at the time the

managing director of a publishing firm called De La Rue. Born in India in 1925 and educated at the Universities of Edinburgh and Cambridge, Shepherd-Barron had his moment of inspiration, in common with so many other great thinkers, while he was lying in the bath.

He had been dwelling on the experience of arriving at his bank on a Saturday morning to cash a cheque, only to find it closed. What was needed, he concluded, was a way of getting hold of your cash wherever and whenever you wanted it. Then his mind turned to chocolate-bar-vending machines and it occurred to him that the same sort of system might be used to dispense cash.

He put his ideas into a formal proposal and approached the chief executive of Barclays Bank, who was immediately taken with the notion. The two men reached an agreement there and then, toasting their new relationship over a pink gin. This being the days before bank cards with magnetic strips, the new machines were built to recognise cheques impregnated with a radioactive substance, carbon-14, which could then be matched to the correct account. Shepherd-Barron initially imagined that the customer's personal identification number (PIN) would be composed of six figures (the same length as his army number) but his wife was able to retain a sequence of only four, which has since become the industry norm.

Having inserted their cheque and entered their PIN, the user could then expect to be presented with a crisp £10 note. To begin with, six pilot machines were installed. The first was in Enfield (north London) and there were others in Hove, Ipswich, Luton, Peterborough and Southend. Of all the people they could have chosen to unveil the Enfield machine on 27 June 1967, Reg Varney was perhaps not the most obvious.

Varney was to be best known for his role as the cheeky-chappie leading man of the hugely popular (and irredeemably un-politically correct) sitcom *On the Buses*. However, that series was still two years away and at the time his fame rested on his role in *Beggar My Neighbour*, in which he played a successful but down-to-earth working-class figure. It was an image no doubt more appealing to Barclays than the one associated with his subsequent performance as a philandering bus driver, prone to occasional minor fraud and proud of his decidedly patchy relationship with authority. In fairness, on the day he became the first man to use a cashpoint, Reg looked most respectable, dressed in smart slacks, a shirt, tie, sweater and dapper white cap.

And, of course, despite some initial problems with

vandalism, ATMs went on to conquer the world. There are estimated to be some 800,000 across the globe, of which 20 per cent are the product of Shepherd-Barron's De La Rue company.

The First Registered Trademark:
The Bass Brewery

If we accept a trademark as being any name or symbol by which a product can be identified, then it is arguable that trademarks came into being virtually concurrently with the start of trade among humans. For instance, there are cave paintings dating back to 5000 BC that include depictions of bison with distinct marks on their sides, which historians assume denote the ownership of the creatures. Similarly, we have archaeological evidence from all of the great ancient civilisations of pottery and stoneware bearing marks to identify either the owners or the manufacturers. Others have convincingly argued that heraldic coats of arms served as a familial trademark, while others hold that assay marks on precious metals were the earliest examples of officially sanctioned trademarks.

However, legislation enshrining the integrity of trademarks is only a relatively recent phenomenon. In 1452, in England there was a case of a widow being granted permission to continue use of her husband's mark. Then, in 1618, again in England, there is the first recorded court case over misuse of a trademark, when two cloth makers (Southern and How) clashed over the alleged adoption of one's mark by the other without permission.

Come the 1790s, Thomas Jefferson was suggesting the need for a legal framework to govern the issue in America, but it was not until 1857 that France took up the challenge and passed the first trademark legislation. Britain followed suit in 1862 and the US in 1870. However, the first acknowledged trademark registry was not established until 1876, when one was set up in Britain following an Act of Parliament the previous year.

The first company to register a mark with the registry, and thus arguably the first official trademark in the world, was that of the Bass Brewery. Established in Burton upon Trent by William Bass in 1777, the company sold its famous Bass Pale Ale to all corners of the British Empire. Its trademark, which lives on today, was one of simple elegance, composed of a solid red triangle. It was assigned the prized registration number '1', and its success and longevity have been an example to marketers the world over who have come to realise that, more often than not, less really is more when it comes to branding.

The title of oldest continuously used trademark has been one particularly fought over by brewing companies, with both Stella Artois (Belgium) and Löwenbräu (Germany) able to trace their insignias back to the second half of the fourteenth century. But, alas for them, it was Bass who can claim the earliest legal recognition.

The First Stock Exchange:
Beursplein, Bruges

The stock market has its origins in Northern Italy during the late Middle Ages, where concepts such as the 'company' and bills of exchange gradually established themselves. But it is to an inn in the then bustling Belgian trade hub of Bruges that we must turn to discover the roots of the first stock exchange.

Bruges got its city charter in 1128. With a comprehensive canal network, by the turn of the fourteenth century, it not only served the Flemish textile industry and the traders of the Northern European Hanseatic League, but had also become a primary destination for merchant fleets coming from Italy.

The Van der Beurse clan was one of the best-known families in the city by then, having been running a guest house from at least 1285. Under the stewardship of Robert Van der Beurse by the early 1300s, the inn sat on

Beursplein (Beurse Square), which was the favoured location for money changers and merchants to carry out their business. The merchants would arrange themselves into 'nation houses', loose associations of dealers from the same country of origin. City natives tended not to be involved in the trades themselves but acted as independent agents going between the various nation houses during 'office hours', thus establishing perhaps the world's first tradition of brokers. This work was particularly well suited to innkeepers, who could make use of any intelligence garnered from the travellers passing through their premises.

While Beursplein was the recognised centre for this type of business, transactions were not formally documented, but proceeded on the basis of custom and tradition. The square was kept clear of vagrants and idlers to ensure the wheels of commerce were not obstructed, and, should the weather be on the unfriendly side, transactions took place under the eaves of the inn or else inside. Business had been going on in this way for many years before the formal establishment of the Beurse in 1309.

Sadly for Bruges, its days as a hub of European trade were to come to an end by the late 1400s, not least because its canals silted up, cutting off access for ships into the city. Bruges was superseded by Antwerp, which boasted the first purpose-built stock exchange in 1531. The influence of Bruges was not to be entirely erased, though, and the Van der Beurse name lives on in the word 'Bourse', still used widely throughout Europe to denote a Stock Exchange.

'He's right, there's no mention here.'

CHAPTER SEVEN

Sport

The First Modern World Heavyweight Boxing Champion: 'Gentleman' Jim Corbett

The brutal fight at the Olympic Club in New Orleans on 7 September 1892, in which Jim Corbett defeated reigning champion John L. Sullivan, signalled the moment when boxing emerged from the illicit underworld of bare-knuckle prize-fighting to become a legitimate modern sport. It was the first world heavyweight title bout to be fought under the Queensberry Rules, which added a sheen of legitimacy to the sport by insisting on certain standards of sportsmanship and introducing measures to ensure the welfare of fighters, including the use of gloves, three-minute rounds and the ten-second knockout rule.

The Queensberry Rules had been codified as early as 1865 by John Graham Chambers in London, England, under the patronage of the Marquess of Queensberry. However, it was to take many years for the code to spread across the Atlantic and to be absorbed by the boxing fraternity. Indeed, Sullivan himself, a proud Irish-American known as the Boston Strong Boy, was a living legend, but personified the dirty old fight game, winning his world title back in 1882 by defeating Paddy Ryan. In 1885, Sullivan won a six-round bout 'to decide the Marquess of Queensberry glove contest for the championship of the world', but it lacked the recognition afforded to the much longer contest he would fight with Corbett.

Overfond of alcohol, Sullivan was never far from trouble and had become America's most famous sportsman by touring the country, playing to packed theatres and offering to take on any comers who fancied their chances against him. He garnered further notoriety by cohabiting with a burlesque entertainer while still married. Dressed in his customary uniform of green tights, brown boots and a loose-fitting white sweater, Sullivan had last defended his title in 1887 in a bare-knuckle bout against Jack Kilrain, which he had won after 75 gruelling rounds.

Corbett, on the other hand, provided a glimpse of

what boxing might be in the future. It was said that he was college-educated and, when not fighting, he held down a job as a bank clerk. His first professional fight was in 1886 and all of his contests were gloved. Well spoken and smartly presented, 'Gentleman' Jim offered a stark contrast to Sullivan. On the fight night, the two pugilists were to battle it out in front of a crowd of 10,000, while news of how the fight was progressing was relayed to bars and clubs throughout the country.

The slugger Sullivan came out strong, but Corbett was perhaps the first great boxing strategist. He allowed his opponent to come at him, using his jab to cleverly work away at Sullivan, who, now 34 years old, was losing his battle against age and overindulgence. In the third round, as the crowd began to barrack Corbett for running, he unleashed his first ferocious attack, smashing Sullivan's nose. The two men rumbled on and, by Round 21, Corbett would later say, he fully expected another 10 or 15 rounds. But then: 'I let my guns go.' and, seeing the champion reeling, went in for the kill. When he crashed his right hand into Sullivan's jaw, the fight was over and 'Gentleman' Jim was world champion.

Sullivan promptly retired but found a new place in the nation's heart. With the championship fight having been for a winner-takes-all purse, Sullivan was not in the best of financial states, but was honoured with a benefit night at Madison Square Garden, at which he undertook some gentle sparring with the new champion. Sullivan eventually gave up the demon drink, even undertaking a lecture tour to publicise its evils, but the damage had been done by then and he died in 1918 aged 59. Corbett lost his title in 1897 to Bob Fitzsimmons but carved out a successful career in the movies and on stage, as well as writing a well-received autobiography. If Sullivan was the last of the prize-fighters, Corbett was the first of the modern professional boxers.

The First Modern Olympic Champion: James Connolly

It was the dream of Frenchman Baron Pierre de Coubertin to re-establish the tradition of the Olympic Games of ancient Greece. He got his wish when the first Modern Olympics were hosted in Athens in 1896. With the USA destined to become its most successful nation in the years to come, it is perhaps fitting that they provided the first champion. That said, James Connolly was far from your average 'jock'.

Born into a poor Irish-American family in Boston, Massachusetts, in 1868, James was one of twelve children. Financial pressures meant he was unable to complete his high-school education, instead joining an insurance company as a clerk to secure a much-needed wage. Despite this disadvantage, his talent – both intellectually and as a sportsman – would not be kept down. A keen footballer and cyclist, he was also an autodidact and in 1895 he successfully sat the entrance exams to study classics at Harvard University.

The prospect of competing at the inaugural Olympics seems to have seized the imagination of Connolly, possibly at the expense of his academic work. He applied to the university for leave to chance his arm at the long jump, high jump and the hop, skip and jump (now called the triple jump). The authorities, though, declined the request, his tutor suggesting that his work did not necessarily merit keeping a place open for him. Connolly would have none of it and decided to quit.

He had to rely on his own savings and some funding from a local athletics club to pay his passage to Greece, travelling first by freighter and then by train. The journey was not without incident, Connolly being robbed of his tickets by a Neapolitan street thief who broke the cardinal rule of mugging: never try to outrun an Olympic athlete. Connolly made it to the Games just in time to compete in the hop, skip and jump, the first final on the first day of the championships. It is said that, having identified his main competitor, he cast his cap a metre beyond their best distance to act as a marker. He then outjumped even that, leaping a gigantic 13.71 metres (45 feet) to secure victory. Medal conventions then being rather different, his first place was rewarded with a silver, as opposed to gold, medal. More importantly, he wrote himself into history as the first Olympic champion since ancient times.

For good measure, he took second place in the high jump and third in the long jump. His attempts to defend his hop, skip and jump in Paris four years later faltered when his compatriot, Meyer Prinstein, edged him out.

Away from athletics, Connolly carved out a highly successful career as an author and journalist, in which capacity he covered the 1904 Games in St Louis (where, incidentally, gold, silver and bronze medals were awarded for the first time). A keen and able sailor, Connolly won particular acclaim for a series of maritime novels and also managed to fit in two unsuccessful campaigns to win a seat in Congress.

Harvard was finally to recognise its former student's gifts, offering him an honorary doctorate many years later, which he no doubt took great satisfaction in turning down. He died in 1957, having achieved vastly more than his humble roots had promised.

The First Grand National Winner: Lottery

Strangely, the first Grand National was arguably the fourth. The famous Aintree racecourse hosted the inaugural 'Great Liverpool Chase' in 1836, which was won by a horse called Duke. However, its organisation was rather haphazard and there is the strong suggestion that the race moved courses to Maghull in the following two years. When it was held at Aintree on 26 February 1839, it was far better managed and had been renamed 'The Grand Liverpool Steeplechase', ensuring that it has come to be regarded as the first running of the Grand National proper (though the 'Grand National Handicap Steeplechase' title did not come into use until 1847).

The 1836 race had been organised by William Lynn, a local hotel owner, but by 1839 it was run by a committee of the racing fraternity's big hitters. Some 50 horses were down to race in the days leading up to the event but in the end 18 contested the course, two laps round a testing cross-country route. All horses were declared as carrying 12 stone.

The favourite, at 6/1, was called The Nun but Lottery, being ridden by one Jem Mason, had decent support at 9/1. Owned by Mr John Elmore, a London horse dealer, Lottery had been trained at the George Dockeray stables in Epsom. One tale is told that Lottery would entertain visitors to the Elmore estate by leaping over the dining table set ready for dinner – a truly unusual training technique. Aged ten in 1839, he was coming into his prime and had a most able companion in Mason (destined to become Dockeray's son-in-law in due course), who wore Elmore's colours of a blue jacket and black cap.

The start was scheduled for 3pm. Two horses formed an early breakaway group, one called Dixon and the other Conrad. Conrad was ridden by Captain Becher, who had been the winner of the 1836 race. However, at the second of two brook jumps, Conrad refused and Becher was deposited in the water. This was to become the most famous jump in the race, and probably the world, having been given the name Becher's Brook. Becher managed to remount his ride, but fell again later in the race.

It was at Becher's Brook on the second time around that Lottery took the lead for the first time and he never looked back. With plenty to spare, Lottery came home in 14 minutes 53 seconds, winning by three clear lengths from the second-placed horse, Seventy Four. Ten horses finished, with The Nun coming seventh after twice dismounting her rider.

Lottery's success continued in 1840, when in a single month he won four out of six steeplechase races at venues scattered around the country. This being the days before 4x4s and horse boxes, he had to be walked to each race. Such was his reputation that one 'open' race, held in Horncastle, specifically invited 'all horses except Mr Elmore's Lottery'.

After a hugely successful eight seasons of racing, Lottery took his bow at Windsor in April 1844 and was honourably retired to stud at Astley Grange Farm in East Langton, Leicestershire. Lottery never forgot Mason, with whom he always had a tempestuous relationship, and, when the jockey paid his old champ a final visit in the late 1840s, Lottery was said to have given him a most ferocious reception.

The First Golf Club: The Gentlemen Golfers of Edinburgh

Variations on golf were being played in the Roman Empire and had certainly made an impact in Scotland by the fifteenth century. So much so that, in 1457, King James II banned the game because he feared it was interfering with his troops' commitment to archery practice. However, it was soon back in royal favour and was a particularly popular pastime of Mary, Queen of Scots. Yet, the rules were not officially formulated until the Gentlemen Golfers of Edinburgh (renamed the Honourable the Edinburgh Company of Golfers in 1800 and, later, as simply the Honourable Company of Edinburgh Golfers) was established in 1744.

The club came about after a group of keen players decided to appeal to Edinburgh's town council for a trophy to be awarded to the winner of a formal competition. The council, which had provided the Royal Company of Archers with the prize of a silver arrow earlier in the century, agreed to supply a silver golf club on condition that the players come up with 'proper regulations' for the game. This they did, devising the 'Articles and Laws in Playing at Golf', which consisted of 13 different rules, neatly set out in the minutes of the meeting at which the club was formally instituted. Its rules would be adopted by the Royal and Ancient Club at St Andrews on its establishment ten years later, thus becoming the code that became standard throughout the world over the decades that followed.

Having satisfied the council's demands, the Edinburgh Golfers held their first 'Annual competition among Noblemen and Gentlemen from any part of Great Britain and Ireland' on 2 April 1744. In reality, the silver trophy was contested by eleven members of the club over ten holes (or two rounds of the Leith Links' five-hole course). A twelfth competitor was a late withdrawal. John Rattray, a local doctor, emerged victorious and was crowned 'Captain of the Golf'.

It is to be supposed that Rattray and his chums celebrated at Luckie Clephan's, their local watering hole of choice. However, in 1767, the Company of Edinburgh Golfers spent the not inconsiderable sum of £767 to build facilities for use by its members. This was, to all intents and purposes, the first '19th hole' in the game. So popular did the course become (combined with some financial difficulties for the club) that they made the decision to up sticks altogether and moved to a new home at Musselburgh in 1836, playing within the boundaries of the famous Edinburgh racecourse. They moved once more in the 1890s to what would become the legendary Muirfield course.

The First Wimbledon Tennis Champion: Spencer Gore

Spencer Gore, born and brought up in Wimbledon in southwest London, became the first men's singles champion of what has become the world's premier tennis tournament in 1877. That said, he could hardly have been more nonplussed by his achievement.

Born in 1850 just down the road from where the tournament was to be held, Spencer William Gore attended Harrow, the famous public school, where he was noted as a very handy footballer and a prodigious cricketing talent, too, captaining the school side. He was also an exceptional player of rackets, a sport that grew up amid the prisons and inns of eighteenth-century

England as, essentially, a cross between tennis and squash. From its roots among the lower echelons of society, it became popular in several of the nation's great schools, and particularly so at Harrow, where an enlarged schoolyard built in the 1820s proved an excellent training ground.

In 1877, the All England Croquet Club at Wimbledon was coming up to its tenth anniversary when it took the momentous decision to branch out and become the All England Lawn Tennis and Croquet Club. Since its inception in 1868, the club had fostered a close relationship with a weekly sporting magazine called *The Field*. Now the publication agreed to sponsor a tennis tournament open to all amateurs on payment of a guinea entry fee. Competitors were to bring their own racket and 'shoes without heels' to play in, while the kindly club gardener would provide the balls. With the enticement of a silver cup valued at 25 guineas, 22 players entered.

The competition began on Monday, 9 July, with the semi-finals due to be completed by the Thursday. There was then to be a break (so as not to be in direct competition with the big draw of the Eton-versus-Harrow cricket match at Lords), with the final scheduled for the following Monday. Gore made it safely through the opening rounds, in matches where the overarm serve was an innovation yet to take hold. In the semi-final he beat C. G. Heathcote to set up a meeting with William Marshall, who had received a bye into the final.

This being Wimbledon, heavy rain struck on the Monday and kept up so that the final was not played until Thursday the 19th, watched by a healthy crowd of 200 who had paid a shilling (5p) each for the privilege. In those gentler times, certain etiquette had to be observed, so players were 'kindly requested not to play in short sleeves when ladies are present'. Just after 4.30pm, Gore claimed victory, having defeated Marshall 6–1, 6–2, 6–4 in just over three-quarters of an hour.

Gore returned the following year to defend his title, but lost the final in three sets to a Mr Frank Hadow, who repeatedly employed a killer lob. It was the last serious competitive tennis that Gore ever played, although it is unlikely he was overly perturbed by that. For a chap who was really rather good at it, he had a distinctly take-it-or-leave-it attitude to the game. Indeed he was to say: 'That anyone who has really played well at cricket, tennis, or even rackets, will ever seriously give his attention to lawn tennis, beyond showing himself to be a promising player, is extremely doubtful; for in all probability the monotony of the game would choke him before he had time to excel in it.'

Alas for Percy, his bid to become a major first-class

cricketer never quite came off. He did make five first-class appearances, including two for Surrey, but, with a batting average of 9.37 and only one wicket to his name, he had to satisfy himself with a career as a capable club player.

The First Motor Racing Champion:
Georges Bouton

Georges Bouton was a talented engineer who, along with the Comte Jules Albert de Dion, was a pioneer of the French motoring industry. De Dion was something of an aristocratic hellraiser with a particular fondness for duelling and a passion for anything mechanical. He first encountered Bouton in 1881 when he visited the shop Bouton co-owned in Léon with his brother-in-law, Charles Trépardoux, to admire the scientific toys built and sold there. The three men shared a dream of building a steam car, and de Dion offered the financial backing to achieve it. By 1883, the relationship had developed so far that the de Dion-Bouton Automobile Company was established.

At the time, there was a popular magazine devoted to, of all things, cycling. It was called *Le Vélocipède* and was edited by the forward-thinking M. Fossier. It was he who decided that the magazine should sponsor a race (strictly speaking, it was a reliability trial) for motor cars over a course of 2 kilometres (1.24 miles) between Neuilly Bridge and the picturesque Bois de Boulogne in Paris. The great spectacle was pencilled in the diary for 28 April 1887.

The visionary M. Fossier perhaps awaited with excitement the daily delivery of the post in the build-up, dreaming of a rush of entries from those daring spirits involved in pioneering the automobile. He was, alas, to be badly let down. Georges Bouton was not only the first to throw his name into the ring, he was also the last.

Nonetheless, a challenge is a challenge and so the 'race' went ahead. Bouton drove one of his own de Dion-Boutons (what else?), which was built at the company's factory in Puteaux, a short distance from the start line. It weighed only some 50kg (110 pounds) and boasted a 1hp engine but, according to witnesses, achieved quite a pace. The result was truly never in doubt.

While Bouton was indisputably the first winner of a motor race, the first *competitive* race did not take place for another seven years, on 22 July 1894. Established by another magazine editor, Pierre Gifard of *Le Petit Journal*, the race set out some strict rules: competitors should race in cars 'with no horse' and vehicles had to be safe, cheap to run and reasonably simple to drive. The course was to cover a challenging 127km (79 miles) from

Paris to Rouen and entry cost 10 francs per car. The winner would claim a 5,000-franc prize.

More than a hundred drivers put down their names, though fewer than 70 made it to a preliminary heat over 50km (31 miles) and, of those, only some 20 or 25 started the main event. In another triumph for the de Dion-Bouton stable, the Comte de Dion came home first, after just short of six-and-a-half hours (including a break for lunch). The race organisers adjudged his vehicle to be rather on the impractical side (contravening one of the main rules), so he was stripped of first place, but the point had been made.

The First FA Cup Scorer: Jarvis Kenrick

Despite attempts in recent years to convince the world that there is somehow more glory in reaching fourth in the league than having a shiny silver cup to show off for your efforts, the FA Cup remains the oldest and grandest domestic cup competition of them all.

The first Football Association Challenge Cup competition was held in the 1871/72 season, at the instigation of the FA secretary, Charles Alcock. The prize on offer was a 46cm-high (18-inch) silver cup, manufactured by Martin, Hall & Co. at a cost of £20. Entry was open to all 50 members of the Association, but only a disappointing 15 signed up, only a few of whom are familiar names today (Barnes, Civil Service, Clapham Rovers, Crystal Palace, Donington School, Hampstead Heathens, Harrow Chequers, Maidenhead, Marlow, Queen's Park, Reigate Priory, Royal Engineers, Upton Park, Wanderers and Windsor Home Park).

The tournament was noted for some pretty shambolic organisation and odd decisions (*plus ça change*, one might say). For instance, Queens Park (based in Glasgow) were given a bye to the semi-finals, as travel was so difficult for them. Games drawn saw both teams through to the next round, Donington School dropped out before kicking a ball in anger and never graced the competition again. The finalists themselves included a team that had won only one tie (having walkovers or achieving draws in the other rounds), and another team that had only drawn their semi-final against Queens Park but went through because Queens Park couldn't afford to travel to the replay.

Such detail must not stand in the way of history, though. In the first round, Clapham Rovers were draw away to Upton Park, with the match played on the afternoon of Saturday, 11 November 1871. After a quarter of an hour, it was all square and evenly balanced. But then up popped Kenrick, who was still two days short of his 19th birthday, to prod home the first goal of the game, and indeed of the whole competition. His place in the annals of the game was assured. His teammate, A. Thompson, fired in a second before half-time and, with ten minutes of the game remaining, Kenrick topped off his man-of-the-match performance with a third for Rovers. Upton Park could conjure up nothing in reply.

Clapham played their second-round game on 16 December, hosting Wanderers at their Clapham Common pitch. This was the archetypal local derby, as Wanderers hailed from Wandsworth. They were the powerhouse of the game in this period and entered the match with well-justified confidence. Rovers – in their customary kit of a cerise and grey shirt, white shorts and black socks – came out in hope rather than expectation. Kenrick was unable to repeat his earlier feats and Wanderers scored in each half to knock Rovers out.

It may have been some consolation to Kenrick and his cohorts when Wanderers swept all before them, winning the inaugural competition by beating the Royal Engineers 1–0 in front of 2,000 spectators at the final at Kennington Oval on 16 March 1872. Kenrick himself proved he was no flash in the pan. Seeing which way the wind was blowing, he went on to join Wanderers, winning the cup with them in 1876, 1877 and 1878. He scored in the 1877 final and got another two in the showpiece the following year. As if all that were not enough, he showed off his prowess at cricket by making a first-class appearance for Surrey in 1876 too. He died in 1949 in Sussex.

The First Man to Hit a Test Match Six:
Joe Darling

One of the greatest players of his generation, Joe Darling played 34 tests for Australia over 11 years. He was the captain of the all-conquering 1902 team that toured England and is remembered as among the greatest of all international sides. But perhaps Joe's finest single moment happened on home soil in the third test of the 1897–98 tour by England. Not only did he become the first man to hit a six in that pressure-cooker environment, but by doing so he notched up a century, one of three he scored in his test career.

Joe was born in 1870 in South Australia. Of compact and powerful build, by his mid-teens, he was displaying considerable sporting prowess, both in Australian Rules football and at cricket, breaking several South Australian schoolboy scoring records. After school and agricultural college, he went to work on his father's farm and in 1893 he married, going on to have 15 children (or a compete XI, an umpire, a scorer and two left over to prepare the tea).

It was in 1894 that he made his test debut, playing against a touring England team. Two years later, he travelled with Australia for the reverse fixtures and toured England again in 1899, 1902 and 1905. But it was the 1897–98 tour that thrust him towards greatness as he achieved a rash of records against a formidable team from the motherland captained by A. E. Stoddart.

Until 1910, it was the rule that a six was awarded only if the batsman hit the ball not simply clean over the boundary, but out of the ground entirely. During the third test at the Adelaide Oval in January 1898, Darling was facing the bowling of Johnny Briggs when he hit to square leg and sent the ball crashing out of the ground, moving his score sweetly from 98 to 104. He went on to repeat the feat twice in his innings, which ended only when he was dismissed for 178. Australia won convincingly by an innings and 13 runs to take a 2–1 lead in the series. They would eventually win 4–1.

By the end of the series, he had become the first man to score three centuries in an Ashes series. In his 160 in the fifth test in Sydney, he racked up the century in a then record 91 minutes. After those efforts, he even had time for a short retirement from the game in 1900 ('in fairness to my wife and children') before returning to captain the glorious 1902 tour to England, where he became the first to hit a six in a test on English soil.

After giving up the game at the highest level in 1905, he moved to a farm in Tasmania in 1908 and continued to play club cricket into his fifties. In 1921, he entered local politics, taking a seat on the Tasmanian Legislative Council, where he remained for the next 25 years. He was awarded a CBE in 1938, and he died in Hobart on 2 January 1946.

The First Rugby Club: Guy's Hospital Rugby Club

It is oft repeated that the game of rugby was born in 1823 when a pupil at Rugby School, William Webb Ellis, 'with a fine disregard for the rules of football as played in his time, first took the ball in his arms and ran with it', as a plaque at the school describes the occasion. The truth of the tale is somewhat doubtful, but this was certainly a period when the rules of football were not yet fixed, with the details usually decided by the captains of opposing teams just before kick-off.

It was not until 1845 that Rugby School took it upon itself to formulate the official rules for the game of rugby, by which time the Guy's club had already been up and running for two years. While there is virtually no first-hand evidence of the early days of the club (perhaps because no one has been able to decipher the handwriting of all those doctors), there is much circumstantial evidence to suggest it was set up by old boys from Rugby, newly arrived in London to commence their medical studies.

Crucially, still in existence is a fixture card for the 1883/84 season, which makes much of the fact that it was the club's 40th-anniversary season. Its assumed foundation date of 1843 has subsequently been acknowledged by both *The Guinness Book of Records* and the Rugby Football Union, making it considerably older than its nearest rival, the Dublin University Football Club, founded in 1854.

Guy's played its matches on London's Blackheath Common during its early years. Indeed, when 1858 saw the formation of the Blackheath Rugby Club (one of the most famous in the English game), the two teams took to sharing dressing-room facilities at the nearby Princess of Wales Hotel. Guy's went on to play a significant role in the forming of the Rugby Union in 1871 and the establishment of a universal rule code. It provided its first international player in 1870, when W. W. Pinching turned out for England, and its last (or perhaps most recent) was Mike Novak, who also played for England, in 1970.

Guy's greatest era was in the 1920s and into the 1930s, when it really did rank among the best in the game. In later years, it struggled to keep up with the demands of an ever more professional sport, and in 1999 merged with two of its oldest rivals, the St Thomas' Hospital Club, founded in 1864, and the King's College Club, established five years later. They fulfil their fixtures today as Guy's, King's and St Thomas' Rugby Club, or GKT for short.

The First English Woman to Swim (and then heroically fail to swim) the Channel: Mercedes Gleitze

There was little in the background of Mercedes Gleitze to suggest that a life of heroic achievement lay ahead. Born in 1900 in Brighton to a baker and a teacher, she spent her childhood between England and Germany, where her grandparents lived. By the time she was in her early twenties, she was working in Westminster as a bilingual secretary and keeping herself fit with long-distance swims in the Thames. In 1923, she spent a then record 10¾ hours continuously swimming the river.

But it was the challenge of the Channel that captured her imagination most. Captain Matthew Webb had been the first to make a successful swim in August 1875. By the autumn of 1927, Mercedes had made seven unsuccessful attempts. Her greatest day, though, was to come on 7 October of that year, when she set out in the icy-cold early hours from Gris Nez in France. A thick fog ensured there were times when her visibility was less than

4.6 metres (5 yards) but Mercedes was guided by a fishing boat, from which her coach, G. H. Allan, fed her grapes, honey and hot drinks to keep up her strength and spirits. She arrived in England, somewhere between South Foreland and St Margaret's Bay, after 15¼ hours. The 12th cross-Channel swimmer (the third woman and first English woman) promptly collapsed, lapsing in and out of consciousness for two hours, thus missing out on seeing the adoring crowds who had gathered to greet her in Folkestone.

Events then conspired to ensure that the glory due to her would be further delayed. Within a week, another woman, Dorothy Logan, achieved the same feat but almost two hours quicker, so setting a new women's record. But the idea of two women making this trip within the space of a week raised many an eyebrow and, folding under the pressure, Logan quickly owned up that her swim had been a hoax. The cruel fallout from her confession saw doubt cast on Gleitze's exploits too. Mercedes's response, courageous and reckless, was to promise to repeat the swim on 21 October. This was what became known as the 'Vindication Swim'.

As she set out at 4.21am, conditions were even colder than they had been a fortnight previously. However, there was no fog this time and she was accompanied by several boats carrying crowds of journalists and well-wishers. By 2.45pm, the icy waters had taken their toll, and Mercedes, on the point of unconsciousness, was dragged aboard her guide boat, seven miles short of her goal. She had failed but, such was the heart she displayed and so impressive her endurance in such testing circumstances, that she was heralded as a hero in the press. Any doubts as to the validity of her 7 October achievement were quickly put aside and her rightful place in the record books was assured.

Something of a celebrity by now (not least because of her link-up with Rolex, who made much of giving her a watch to wear during the Vindication Swim that had kept perfect time in the water), Mercedes went on to achieve many other incredible swimming feats. For instance, in 1928 she became the first person to conquer the Straits of Gibraltar and she was also the first to swim from Cape Town to Robben Island and back. In 1932, she set the British record for endurance swimming at 46 hours and then decided to retire.

Gleitze was not only a phenomenal athlete but had a strong social conscience too, using the wealth she gained from swimming to set up a charitable organisation providing accommodation for destitute men and women. She died in London in 1981.

'There's going to be a pretty hefty fine on that.'

CHAPTER EIGHT

The Social Fabric

The First Holiday Camp: Cunningham Camp, Isle of Man

The holiday camp is a peculiarly British notion, at once conjuring up images of fun and freedom alongside prison-style regimentation. Early holiday camps tended to be run by worthies intent on doing some good for the world, and in particular the working classes. This sense was perhaps best encapsulated in one of the earliest successful camps, Dodd's Socialist Camp, which was set up at Caister, near Great Yarmouth, in 1906. The proprietor, Fletcher Dodd, was a well-connected fellow and he attracted the likes of George Bernard Shaw and the Labour Party grandee Kier Hardy to fun and frolic alongside the great unwashed.

But Dodd was following a pattern that had first been tried back in 1894 by a Liverpudlian baker, Joseph Cunningham, and his wife Elizabeth. They established their camp on the Isle of Man and catered exclusively for men, who stayed under candlelit canvas and endured pretty basic conditions. The Cunninghams were devout Presbyterians and had been involved in running youth summer camps in Liverpool's down-on-its-uppers Toxteth area. They had initially administered the project in partnership with a local charitable organisation, the Florence Institute, but, after a fractious relationship, the Cunninghams decided to go it alone.

Having hit upon what they considered the perfect location at Howstrake, a couple of miles from Douglas, capital of the Isle of Man, they opened up the resort to some 600 men per week, charging them a princely 10 shillings (50p) for the privilege. The regime they imposed was far removed from the knobbly-knees and kiss-me-quick culture championed by the likes of Billy Butlin during the golden age of the holiday camp that lasted from the 1930s to the 1960s. There was strictly no women, alcohol or gambling, and hell to pay should any holidaymaker dare break the curfew (11.45pm Monday–Saturday and 10.30pm on Sundays).

However, the punters kept on coming, so the Cunninghams must have been doing something right.

Everyone was encouraged to partake in team games and singsongs, and various amenities were added over the years until the camp was the rival of many high-class hotels. Visitors were free to make use of a heated swimming pool and could visit the onsite barber, bank, bakery or concert hall. Sumptuous meals were served in the dining room, with many ingredients coming from the camp's own associated farm. There was even its own publication, *The Camp Herald*.

The low prices charged by the Cunninghams had always caused friction with the other, more expensive, hotels on the island and the camp came under attack very quickly after it opened, with accusations that it was far too conducive to loose morals. In an agreement with the local authorities, the tents gradually gave way to more permanent buildings. It thus came to have some of the earliest versions of holiday chalets, the bedrock of so many later camps. By the turn of the twentieth century, the Cunninghams were hosting 1,500 people at a time, and in 1904 the proprietors sought a new base, moving to the Falcon Cliff area of the island.

The camp was used to house enemy aliens during the First World War and as a military training camp during the Second World War. During peacetime, though, it continued to thrive and remained in the family until the late 1940s.

The First Zoo: Hierakonpolis

To the modern mind, a zoo is a collection of wild or non-native animals kept in captivity and available for visitation by the public, often with educational or ecological goals in mind. London Zoo, which opened in 1828 as the collection of the Zoological Society of London, was the first institution to be called such, its predecessors largely known by the term 'menagerie'. Menageries had grown increasingly popular from the Enlightenment onwards, when collections of wild animals were put on display for the amusement and education of society at large, often organised on a rather less scientific basis than would be deemed acceptable today. Among the most famous of all menageries, and widely regarded as the forerunner of the modern zoo, was the Imperial Menagerie at the Schönbrunn Palace in Vienna, a gift to the people from the Hapsburg monarchy, which opened in 1752.

However, in 2009, a team of archaeologists at Hierakonpolis, the derelict city that was once the capital of Upper Egypt, suggested that they had found evidence of the world's first known zoo, operating as long ago as 3500 BC. Settled around 4000 BC, Hierakonpolis sat on the River Nile just south of Luxor and was the land's political and cultural heart. It has been the subject of extensive archaeological exploration for several decades now. The expedition leader, Dr Renee Friedman, announced that her team had discovered an extraordinary array of more than a hundred animal skeletons.

The collection included hippopotamuses, elephants, baboons, dogs, cats, wildcats and a hartebeest (a type of antelope). Many were buried in the tombs of powerful rulers, having presumably been sacrificed on the master's death. It is probable that these animals were not merely symbolic of royal power wielded over the beasts of the earth, but may well have represented certain characteristics that a king might desire to adopt in death.

Yet there is much evidence to suggest that these animals, many of which were certainly not natural inhabitants of the region, were kept to be more than merely funereal sacrifices. Friedman in particular pointed to the fact that an elephant had stomach contents containing cultivated and non-native plants (wheat chaff, acacia twigs and river plants related to papyrus), suggesting that the creature was being fed a specially prepared diet. Other animals displayed fractures that could have healed only in a protected environment.

While there is no suggestion that these animals were on public display or were kept with any benevolent educational or ecological intentions, they do represent at least one ruler's personal collection of exotic species, moved to the city and nurtured in captivity. Whatever the reason for this, the remarkable menagerie at Hierakonpolis can lay claim to being the first zoo in history.

The First Librarian: Ibnisarru of Agade

It is to be assumed that, as soon as mankind began written communication, there were gathered together collections of these communications that might in some sense be regarded as libraries (for what *is* a library if not a collection of written materials?). In an age before transportable books, writing was often done by making inscriptions in surfaces such as walls, so we might even consider an ancient cave or inscribed tomb as a sort of library.

But the first library of which we have evidence, in terms of a place where transportable texts were brought together, is the Great Library of Agade. Agade (also known as Akkad) was one of the great cities of antiquity, located in modern-day Iraq between the rivers Euphrates and Tigris and believed to have been established by Sargon I, who lived from roughly 2300 to 2215 BC. He created a vast empire (known as the Akkadian Empire) by conquering numerous city-states of the Sumerian civilisation, which he ruled from his Agade power base. Although the city has yet to be accurately located and excavated by archaeologists, we know he established a library there that employed a librarian (the first such professional that we know of) by the name of Ibnisarru.

Ibnisarru's seal and a section of the library catalogue have remarkably found their way down to us, and from these historians have been able to paint a picture of an operation similar in many details to the types of library we have today. Every visitor to the library was presented with a piece of papyrus on to which they were to put their name and the details of the text they wished to view. Ibnisarru (or whoever happened to be on duty) would then look out the relevant tablet, for this was long before the age of the printed book, and present it to the borrower. Tablets were stored for ease of use under classifications that evolved over the lifespan of the library, just as we have now.

The next great library for which there is rather more significant archaeological evidence was built at Mari (modern-day Tel Al-Hariri in Syria). In 1933, an archive was unearthed containing around 23,600 clay tablets. They were inscribed with cuneiform script, one of the earliest-known writing systems that emerged in the Sumerian world around 3000 BC, and have been dated to between 2285 and 1755 BC. On that basis, it is not inconceivable that the libraries at

Mari and Agade might have been established almost contemporaneously.

The First Scout Troop: The 1st Glasgow Scouts

Robert Baden-Powell was born in Paddington, London, in 1857 and began a distinguished military career in 1876. Spending much of his time with the army in southern Africa, he achieved national fame during the Second Boer War as he led the resistance during the Siege of Mafeking from 1899 to 1900. During this heroic episode, he made much use of a cadet corps of brave guards and messengers composed of boys not yet old enough to fight.

Recollections of the corps featured in Baden-Powell's best-selling military training manual, *Aids to Scouting*, written in 1901. Many existing youth movements took the work to their hearts and the leader of the Boys Brigade, Sir William Smith, gave particular encouragement to Baden-Powell and his ideas. Spurred on, Baden-Powell decided to run a test camp for 20 boys in August 1907 on Brownsea Island, an idyllic hideaway that lies in Poole Harbour off the south coast of England.

With the experience of what was in effect the first Scout camp fresh in his mind, he set about rewriting *Aids to Scouting* for a younger readership, and published it as a part-work, *Scouting for Boys*, in January 1908. It was an immediate phenomenon and a wave of Scout patrols sprang up across the nation. By April, an office had been established to focus on the needs of the new patrols and it was not long before Baden-Powell gave up his own military career to focus on the Scouting movement.

Such was the speed of growth that administration inevitably lagged behind and the Scouting Association has no definitive record of the first troop to be established. However, the 1st Glasgow troop has the earliest verified registration certificate, retrospectively dated for 26 January 1908. The troop itself would seem to have been established ten days before that, rising phoenix-like from the dissolved Glasgow Battalion of the Army Cadet Corps.

That battalion had been established the previous June by Captain Robert E. Young (or 'Boss' Young, as he was known) and was a roaring success, training the lads in the intricacies of knot tying and signalling, and always concluding with a 'good tuck-in'. Its initial membership came from four local schools: Glasgow Academy, Kelvinside Academy, Glasgow High School and Hillhead High School. Young then met Baden-Powell, who suggested the group might make use of *Scouting for Boys*. So popular was it that Young decided to reform the group, arranging for the Scouts to meet at a ground-floor flat at 6 Strathallan Street. Young was eternally popular with the boys who passed through the troop and he remained in charge of it until his death in 1940. The troop continues to prosper to this day.

The First Person to be Cremated in a Crematorium: Alberto Keller

There is evidence that humans have disposed of their dead by burning for at least 20,000 years, but the practice all but died out (if the pun may be excused) in Europe after the rise of Christianity. Indeed, so looked down upon was it that for much of the Middle Ages the only people who were cremated were heretics or others considered deserving of the most terrible punishments. However, changing ideas about the nature of the soul allied with pressing practical concerns about overpopulated graveyards in urban spaces saw the rise of a movement in favour of cremation during the nineteenth century.

By the 1870s, there was a real groundswell in support of the notion, spearheaded by the likes of a campaigning professor from Padua called Brunetti. As a result, cremation was legalised in Italy in 1874. On 22 January of that year, a wealthy Milanese resident by the name of

Alberto Keller passed away, leaving 50,000 francs in his will for the construction of a crematorium in Milan's main cemetery. Where other cultures with a tradition of cremation, such as Hinduism, tended to construct pyres on an as-needed basis, this was to be the first purpose-built crematorium.

Keller's body was embalmed and deposited in his family tomb while the design of the crematorium was finalised by Messrs Clericetti and Polli. Having perfected the technology, they constructed a building in the style of a Roman temple, standing on about 4.6 square metres (50 square feet) of land. In the interior of the sarcophagus were 217 gas jets. Beneath its impressive dome roof was a plaque inscribed: 'Cremation Temple, donated, at the desire of the noble Alberto Keller, to the City of Milan'.

After testing of the crematorium's functionality by disposing of the bodies of assorted animals, it was decided to dispatch the first human there on Saturday, 22 January 1876. It was to be Alberto Keller himself, on the second anniversary of his death. The time was set for 2pm. A large throng attended, including the building's designers, the Keller family, local officials, and scientists and journalists from throughout Europe. At the designated hour, Keller's body ('as natural as the day on which it was entombed', according to a newspaper report) was taken from the family casket and transferred to a thin wooden box. A few words were said by a clergyman from Keller's own Evangelical Church before the body was sent into the flames, which burned at a 1000 degrees Celsius. After 45 minutes, the gas jets were turned off, Keller having achieved in death what he most desired in life.

The First Public Park: Birkenhead Park

Often considered the last great Egyptian pharaoh, Ramses III famously provided his citizenry with plentiful and elaborate open spaces during the twelfth century BC. Into the modern age, Városliget (City Park) in Budapest was donated by its owners, the Batthyány family, for the enjoyment of the wider Hungarian public in 1808. Yet it was the rather humbler Birkenhead Park on Merseyside that can claim to be the first truly public park, on the basis that it was created for the public by public funding. Of spectacular design, it was to go on to have a considerable influence on arguably the most famous park in North America.

Birkenhead was thrust into the industrial age with the arrival of the steam ferry in the 1820s, and its population grew from around 100 to more than 2,500 within ten years. Such rapid expansion brought its own problems, and in 1833 the Birkenhead Improvement Commission was created by Act of Parliament. The 'Parks Movement' was by then a powerful voice in the country, advocating the provision of open spaces for the good of the working classes, and in 1841, a Liverpool councillor called Isaac Holmes suggested one be opened in Birkenhead.

William Somerville Jackson showed tremendous determination in driving the project forward while he was chairman of the Birkenhead Commissioners from 1842 to 1846. In 1843 he instigated the purchase of 125 acres of low-grade land from a Mr F. R. Price, and Joseph Paxton was engaged as architect for a fee of £800. Two-thirds of the land was to be for public use and a third for private housing, which would be sold to recoup all the costs of the public park.

Paxton had won fame for several of his designs in the region, most notably Princes Park in Liverpool. He had in mind for Birkenhead the creation of an idealised landscape of woodlands interspersed with meadows. Although he was dubious about the quality of the land designated for the project, he was up for the challenge, considering that 'it will rebound more to my credit and honour to make something handsome and good out of bad materials'.

Paxton employed Edward Kemp to oversee the day-to-day running of the works and eventually Kemp became Park Superintendent. Lewis Hornblower, a youthful local architect, was put in charge of the construction of lodges and various other special features. Among those who laboured in the park were prisoners of war captured during Britain's conflicts with France. Major planting was undertaken during the autumn and spring of 1844 and 1845, with the park ready to open its gates by the end of the following year.

The official opening ceremony was conducted on 5 April, Easter Monday, 1847 by Lord Morpeth, and at least 10,000 people passed through on that day alone. Birkenhead Park Cricket Club, founded in 1846, was given permission to use the park as its home venue and a camera obscura, tearoom and suspension bridge over the lake were all added before the decade was out. In 1850, it was visited by the American architect Frederick Law Olmsted, who observed that 'in democratic America there was nothing to be thought of as comparable with this People's Garden'. He was struck enough that he incorporated several ideas from his visit into his drawings for New York's Central Park.

The First Package Holiday: Loughborough to Leicester (and Back Again)

It may not do for the sun-hungry holidaymakers of the twenty-first century, but, when Thomas Cook organised an improving, all-expenses-paid trip across the Midlands in 1841, he opened the door to a new way of life and began a multibillion-pound global industry.

Although his name is one of the most famous in the tourist trade, it was by no means obvious that Cook was destined to found the travel-agency business when he was born in the Derbyshire village of Melbourne on 22 November 1808. He started his working life aged just ten with a market farmer, before becoming apprenticed as a cabinetmaker in his early teens. By the time he was 20, he was a Baptist minister with a deep sense of moral rectitude and interests in publishing religious pamphlets.

In 1832, he moved to Market Harborough and the following year married. At virtually the same time, he took a pledge of temperance and became a prominent figure in the local anti-alcohol movement. It was while he was walking the not inconsiderable distance from Market Harborough to a temperance meeting in Leicester in 1841 that 'the thought suddenly flashed across my mind as to the practicability of employing the great powers of railways and locomotion for the furtherance of social reform'. His big idea, which he shared with fellow members of the movement, was to charter a train from the Midland Counties Railway Company for the exclusive use of supporters travelling from Leicester to an upcoming meeting in Loughborough, a journey just short of 12 miles. The gathering was scheduled for 5 July 1841.

Having reached agreement with the railway managers, he set about advertising the privately chartered train to the public, the first time anyone had undertaken such a scheme. Five hundred and seventy passengers signed up, paying a shilling (5p) for a return ticket plus food and drink. So successful did it prove that Cook embarked on a period of what he called 'enthusiastic philanthropy', arranging trips for Sunday schools and Temperance Society members throughout the Midlands over the next three summers.

All of this he undertook on a not-for-profit basis, but things changed in 1845, when he ran a pleasure trip from Leicester to Liverpool, advertised with a brochure and costing a princely 10 shillings (50p) per person (or 15 shillings (75p) in first-class). From there, things spiralled. His company took a reputed 150,000 visitors to the Great Exhibition in 1851 and was arranging trips to the Continent by 1855. Within a short while, this had turned into an accompanied Grand Tour of Europe, with America joining the company's portfolio in 1865. In 1872, Cook led the first of the round-the-world tours that kept him away from home (and his two temperance hotels) for a full 222 days and covered more than 25,000 miles.

A London office opened during the 1860s, a short while after Thomas had brought his son, John, into the fold. But the two feuded often and Cook Sr took the decision to retire in 1879. Socially aware till the last, he died in 1892, a year after building a row of cottages in Melbourne for the use of the 'poor and deserving persons belonging to the general Baptist denomination'. Today, Thomas Cook travellers number 6 million per year.

The First University: The University of Bologna

In the ancient world, seats of learning were established principally as centres of religious knowledge or to produce administrators to look after the interests of the ruling class. Such motivations were still prominent in medieval Europe, with the University of Bologna owing its foundation around 1088 to a growing need for skilled lawyers throughout the Continent. Despite the lack of any formal foundation documentation, this is traditionally considered the moment when the masters of grammar, rhetoric and logic adjusted the focus of their teachings to the subject of canon and civil law, freely and independently of the ecclesiastical schools in Bologna.

There were, as you might expect, several older establishments than Bologna that had many of the characteristics of universities, such as the one at Taxila in modern-day Pakistan, which operated in the seventh century BC and offered formal higher academic qualifications. Others have suggested that monasteries of all religions throughout the world had long been operating academic centres that were the natural forefathers of universities.

But Bologna was the first institution to refer to itself specifically as a 'universitas' at its foundation, from the Latin '*universitas magistrorum et scholarium*', to mean an academic community of teachers and scholars. Its focus on disseminating knowledge of Roman law was particularly valuable at a time when Europe was in constant flux as local, state and church interests weighed against each other. Students reputedly came from all corners of Europe as well as North Africa and the Middle East to take advantage of the teachings of such notable masters as Irnerius, who was perhaps the leading name at the time of the university's foundation and is considered to have revolutionised the nature of legal study.

That Bologna was independent of political and religious patronage allowed it an independence and autonomy that has been the hallmark of all the great universities that followed it. In addition, it was the first institution to award a degree in the modern sense (indeed, until recent years, its doctorate of law was the only degree that it granted).

In 1158, the university adopted an edict from the

Holy Roman Emperor Frederick I called *Constitutio Habita*, which protected the rights of scholars to travel unhindered in the interests of furthering education and theoretically guaranteed the university's academic freedom – a landmark moment in the history of European universities. Among Bologna's alumni are such spectacular names as Dante Alighieri, Nicolaus Copernicus, Albrecht Dürer and, in more recent times, Umberto Eco.

'Think of the glory man...the first thespian to play a horse's arse.'

CHAPTER NINE

Entertaiment

The First Circus Ringmaster: Philip Astley

While the famous circuses of ancient Rome did a fine line in wild animals, chariot races and battle re-enactments, the circus as we know it today – with its heady mix of clowns, trained animal acts, acrobats, trapeze artists and the like – can trace its history back to 1768. The man generally acknowledged as establishing the first modern circus was Philip Astley, a celebrated cavalryman who developed his relatively straightforward horse-riding act into a grand spectacle that established a blueprint for the art form.

Astley was born on 8 January 1742 in Newcastle-under-Lyme, the son of a cabinetmaker. Young Philip grew into a strapping 6-foot lad and, at 17 years of age, signed up with the 15th Light Dragoons. He proved adept at breaking in horses and served with distinction in the Seven Years War. It was said that he saved a horse that had fallen overboard in Hamburg, rescued the badly wounded Duke of Brunswick on the battlefield, and claimed the enemy's standard at the battle of Emsdorf. When he left the Dragoons in 1766, having married one Patty Jones the previous year, he was presented with a grey regimental charger called Gibraltar.

After a stint as a groom at the riding school of Mr and Mrs Sampson in Islington, in 1768 Astley set up his own school at Ha'penny Hatch on Lambeth Marsh. There he developed his act as the English Hussar, with a repertoire of daring stunts, including jumping from moving horse to moving horse, straddling two horses at once and doing headstands on a horse's back. Crucially, he realised that, if his horses could continuously canter round a circular 'ring', he could manipulate the qualities of centrifugal force to wow his audiences further. The first show at what he called 'The Royal Grove' was held on 9 January 1768. He charged a shilling (5p) for a seat (or half-price to stand), and the spectacle proved a huge hit, bringing in anything up to 40 guineas a night.

Such popularity drove Astley to add further wonders to his entertainment. There was most certainly a strongman by the name of Signor Colpi, a pair of clowns called

Fortunelly and Burt, a high-wire act and plenty of acrobats. The highlight for many years was an act called 'Billy Buttons', in which a calamitous tailor attempted to ride his horse to Brentford to vote in an election. With plenty of slapstick, it was perhaps the original orchestrated circus clown act. In addition, Astley reinvested some of his profits to put a canvas roof atop the ring, thus creating the forerunner of the modern Big Top.

By 1783, Astley had expanded on to the Continent, opening the Amphithéâtre Anglais in Paris. Several other European franchises followed, including the Equestrian Theatre Royal in Dublin in 1788. In 1804, he was imprisoned in France after a lull in Britain's struggles with Napoleon came to an abrupt end, but he made a dramatic escape back to England. His financial fortunes went through several peaks and troughs, not least when fire claimed his London base on more than one occasion and because of the relative failure of his Olympic Pavilion, which he opened just off the Strand in 1806. He died on 20 October 1814, suffering from gout, which may suggest that he had found at least some time for personal indulgence in his remarkable life.

Ironically, while it was Astley who established the modern circus ring, the big top and the bill of acts so familiar today, he himself never referred to his show as a circus. Instead, it was one of his former employees,

Charles Hughes, who established a rival show in London and called it the Royal Circus.

The First Actor: Thespis

Unlike anybody else in this book, there is some debate as to whether the subject of this entry ever really existed. However, no lesser authority than Aristotle wrote of his life and there is much evidence to suggest Thespis was indeed a real man. Regardless, the figure of Thespis lives on through our tradition of referring to actors as thespians.

Thespis is believed to have been born in the ancient Greek province of Icaria sometime during the sixth century BC. Aristotle, writing long after the death of Thespis, depicted him as a singer of dithyrambs (hymns sung in honour of Dionysus, the god of wine and pleasure). Thespis's great contribution to the acting world was his move away from the purely choral tradition by the addition of prologues and speeches delivered as if by the characters themselves. That is to say, he was the great innovator of acting a role. It was also said that he did much to promote the use of stage sets, costumes, makeup and masks.

In 534 BC, Athens was under the rule of the despotic Pisistratus, who decreed that there should be a 'City Dionysia', a festival in honour of Dionysus. Prizes were to be given to the outstanding performers in various art forms. Thespis wowed the crowds with his poetry performances given in the guises of various characters from atop a wooden cart, which he dragged around with him. He was awarded the festival's first prize and thus established himself as the first acknowledged actor in history.

Alas, very little detail of what Thespis performed has been passed down to us and the knowledge that we do have is heavily disputed. Nor were all his contemporaries great fans. Plutarch reported how the statesman and fellow poet, Solon, demanded of Thespis whether he felt shame at telling such lies to people (acting being, essentially, a grand deception). When Thespis defended his right to entertain, Solon hit the ground with his stick and muttered, 'If we are so pleased with this sort of entertainment, we shall soon find it in public affairs also.' Some may well argue that he had a valid point!

John Dryden, though, was happier to acknowledge his great contribution in the seventeenth century, immortalising him in verse:

Thespis, the first professor of our art,
At country wakes sang ballads from a cart.

The First Man on Television: William Taynton

In an era when every Tom, Dick and Harry thinks not only is it their right to appear on the goggle-box but also that somehow the world will benefit as a result, it is refreshing to think that the first TV 'star' was plucked from utter obscurity to reluctantly play a role at one of the most important moments in modern cultural history.

The race to master the invention of television was battled out frantically by a number of inventors in disparate locations around the world. From late in the nineteenth century, there was a belief that 'television' – the transmission and reception of moving images via electric or electromagnetic signals – was distinctly possible. But who would be the first to demonstrate it in public?

The answer, it would turn out, was John Logie Baird, an engineer from Dunbartonshire in Scotland, born in 1888. Having had his studies at Glasgow University interrupted by the onset of the First World War, Baird never actually graduated, but his technical brilliance was undoubted. That said, by the early 1920s, Baird, a rather sickly figure, was short of money and seemingly far from achieving his dream of perfecting a television system.

By 1924, though, he was able to demonstrate to a select group of journalists his first major breakthrough – the transmission of moving images, albeit in silhouette. He demonstrated his system to the public for the first time at one of London's great stores, Selfridges, in the spring of 1925. The new challenge was to transmit greyscale images so that the viewer could see a picture with defined features rather than a simple silhouette. This he was to achieve at his workshop on 2 October 1925.

Having extensively tested his all-new light-sensitive transmission system, the inventor took a ventriloquist's dummy he had been using in his experiments and transmitted an image of its head. Stooky Bill (for that was the doll's name) usually appeared on Baird's receiving screen as little more than a pale blob with black spots where his facial features were. This time, though, he saw a far more detailed image. Indeed, Baird would recall the 'almost unbelievable clarity'.

Now came Taynton's big moment. Baird's workshop was above some offices where the 20-year-old Taynton served as the errand boy for one Mr Cross. Baird, caught up in the moment, ran downstairs and grabbed the unwitting lad, persuading him to go upstairs and position himself before what must have been a bewildering array of equipment. Baird took himself off to the adjoining room to see if he could replicate the detailed depiction of Stooky Bill with a real human. The immediate answer was 'no'.

He then discovered that Taynton, overcome by the heat and light from the intense lamps Baird used in his setup, had repositioned himself just out of focus. Realising this was a time for bribery, Baird slipped him a half-crown (12½p) on condition that he remain just where Baird wanted him. The boy did as he was told and, sure enough, a detailed image was rendered. William Taynton was television's first star.

After some work to improve the scan rate of his images, Baird publicly demonstrated the new system in front of the Royal Institution in late January 1926. Able to secure new funding on the back of his success, he moved to bigger premises in London. He rewarded Taynton for his role by taking him on as his own office boy. Baird continued his work in the medium, playing a pivotal role in the ongoing improvement of television quality.

The First Feature Film: *The Story of the Kelly Gang*

While Hollywood is, of course, the true capital of the movie-making business, the first full-length feature film was produced in the suburbs of Melbourne, Australia, back in 1906. Its subject was the ruthless bush-ranging killer and national folk hero Ned Kelly.

Ned Kelly famously died in 1880 in a shootout with

police outside the Glenrowan Hotel while wearing a suit of homemade armour, having led his gang on an orgy of thieving and violence that struck at the heart of the colonial authorities. This was material rich for filmmaking. And so it occurred to Charles Tait, a film exhibitor. Tait turned to his brothers, John and Nevin, and two professional colleagues, Millard Johnson and William Gibson, to come up with the financing and co-produce the movie.

Frank Mills was drafted in to star as Ned, while Elizabeth Tait played his sister Kate and Nicholas Brierley took the role of trusty gang member Joe Byrne. Charles Tait wrote the script and was also the director. With a budget of just over $2,000, Tait came up with a film running to a then unprecedented 60 minutes, at a time when the average 'feature' lasted no more than 10.

The Story of the Ned Kelly Gang had its world premiere at the Athenaeum Hall in Melbourne on Boxing Day 1906. While some loved it, others were appalled by its celebration of a violent outlaw. This response was, naturally enough, particularly prevalent in areas where Ned Kelly had been active less than 30 years previously, and indeed the film was subjected to a state-wide ban in Victoria in 1912.

Nonetheless, it was a roaring commercial success. At

least six prints of the film were in circulation and it played to packed houses throughout the country for several weeks. The following year, it transferred to New Zealand and then toured to Ireland and the UK, where it was billed as 'the longest film ever made'. The producers were recompensed for their contributions towards the initial budget many times over and became very rich men indeed. Alas, no complete reels of the film have remained intact. Instead, cinema detectives have been forced to reconstruct passages from film fragments found in various collections around the world and by analysing contemporary reviews. Thus far, only 17 minutes have been restored.

The First Modern Pantomime Director: Augustus Harris

The pantomime we know today – a Christmas treat retelling old fairytales and replete with low-rent celebrity stars, groan-inducing comedy, audience participation, women playing boys and men playing old women – has been an awful long time in the making. The original pantomimes, entirely unrelated to the modern spectacle, were performed in ancient Greece and Rome by travelling players. It can then trace its roots through the hugely popular *comedia dell'arte*, which swept through Italy and France in the fifteenth and sixteenth centuries, and on through the British harlequinades of the eighteenth and nineteenth centuries.

By the mid-nineteenth century, several elements of the modern panto were in place, innovations driven primarily by the fierce competition that raged between London's Drury Lane Theatre and Lincoln's Inn Field Theatre. Many of the popular stories were by then regularly performed (*Cinderella*, for instance, was debuted in 1804) and the scripts of E. L. Blanchard played with the formerly rigid structures of the harlequinade, bringing in bright rhyming verse and topical comedy. Blanchard was the Drury Lane's resident writer from 1852 and he did much to cement the role of the principal boy and the dame. From 1869, the much-loved Vokes family appeared year after year to perform his creations.

Then, in 1879, Augustus Harris, the 28-year-old Paris-born son of an English dramatist and a costume designer, took over at the helm of Drury Lane. And he was armed with a new broom. While the Drury Lane panto had been doing quite nicely, there was a certain sense of stagnation. One critic had described the performance of the Vokeses in 1878 as 'sublimely indifferent' and Blanchard himself seemed to be losing some of the joy, reporting in 1881 that writing his 'annuals' (as he called the pantos) were 'not pleasant work as it used to be'. Although he hung on for several more years, he ultimately gave way to J. Hickory Wood.

Harris was determined to add some razzmatazz to proceedings and bring his shows right up to date, convinced, quite rightly, that the panto was the ultimate populist medium. For starters, in an age where a turned piano leg was enough to leave all and sundry scandalised, he knew that there was significant appeal to an art form where women could legitimately appear in tights, wander around and slap their thighs.

Among his first actions was to quietly sideline the Vokeses and, in a completely new move, use leading music-hall stars instead. In came the likes of Arthur Roberts, Vesta Tilley and the legendary Marie Lloyd. Most successful of all was his inspired partnering of Dan Leno and Herbert Campbell, a much-loved comedy double act destined to become legends of the panto world. Harris was also keen on playing up the 'spectacle' element of his productions, lavishing previously unknown budgets of up to £8,000 per show to fill his stage with grand processions, often comprising numbers in the hundreds. No technical innovation, new act or popular novelty seemed to fall beneath his radar. Virtually all ties to the grand tradition of the harlequinade were removed and there was no pretence to high culture. He wanted bums on seats and that meant crude jokes, outrageous costumes, famous names, topical skits and audience participation. Little has changed in the subsequent hundred and more years.

A character of unbounded energy, Harris was also the owner of the *Sunday Times* for a period and was active in the politics of London, which secured him a knighthood in 1891. He was, though, not to make old bones and died on 22 June 1895, the victim of a wasting disease. 'Augustus Druriolanus', as he was widely known, was justly commemorated as the creator of the modern panto.

The First Man to Reject an Oscar:
Dudley Nichols

The crowning achievement for most of those working in the motion-picture industry is to receive an Academy Award, more commonly known as an Oscar. And you can be sure that anyone willing to turn one down feels they have very good reason. Marlon Brando famously refused his award for Best Actor for *The Godfather* in 1972 in protest at what he regarded as Hollywood's negative depiction of native Americans. A year earlier, George C. Scott had turned down one for his role in *Patton*, describing the whole shindig as 'demeaning' and a 'two-hour meat parade'. However, it was a screenwriter, Dudley Nichols, who was the first to reject the greatest prize in show business, way back in 1936.

Born in 1895 in Ohio, Nichols served with distinction in the First World War before embarking on a career as a journalist in New York. He did not arrive in Hollywood until 1929 but was soon working alongside the great directors of the day, such as Howard Hawks, Fritz Lang and John Ford. It was for the last of these that he wrote the script for *The Informer*, based on Liam O'Flaherty's tale of the struggle for independence in 1920s Ireland. The film was much lauded on its release in 1935 and was showered with awards by the Academy at the 1936 Oscars. Ford was named best director, Victor McLaglen was best actor and Max Steiner won for his musical score. Nichols himself was successful in the screenplay category.

Nichols, though, was highly politicised and at the time he was kicking against Hollywood's overwhelmingly powerful studio system, demanding the right to set up independent unions for actors, directors and screenwriters. In the course of the struggle, Nichols vilified the Academy of Motion Picture Arts and Sciences for establishing 'company unions' that he believed were weak and served only the wishes of the monstrous studios.

In 1933, independent guilds for actors and screenwriters were set up in competition to the 'company unions' (the directors' guild did not follow until 1936), and the two sides were on bad terms. In the build-up to the 1936 ceremony, held on 5 March, high-profile stars such as Gary Cooper and Jimmy Cagney were urging a boycott but were countered by the all-powerful studio bosses, who demanded that their contracted stars not stay away.

As is often the way in Tinseltown, money talks and the boycott largely failed. However, Nichols and, to a lesser extent, Ford were not cowed. Both were absent from the ceremony, although Ford denied it was a snub, saying, 'If I had planned to refuse it, I would not have allowed my name to go in for nomination.'

Nichols was far more outspoken. Never interested in underplaying the importance of the writer in the movie business, he once proclaimed, 'I devoutly believe it is the writer who has matured the medium of film more than anyone else in Hollywood.' Now he posted back the award that was sent to him *in absentia* and told Frank Capra, then president of the Academy, that 'to accept it would be to turn my back on nearly a thousand members who ventured everything in the long-drawn-out fight for a genuine writers' organisation'. Capra promptly returned the Oscar to him, and back it came from Nichols.

If Nichols feared his career would struggle afterwards, he need not have worried. He would go on to work on such acclaimed and successful movies as *Bringing Up Baby, Stagecoach, For Whom the Bell Tolls* and *And Then There Were None*. He also received Oscar nominations in 1940, 1943 and 1957, for *The Long Voyage Home, Air Force* and *The Tin Star*, respectively. In 1937 and 1938, he served as president of the Writers' Guild, when it won legal recognition as the sole bargaining representative for film writers. With the battle between the Guild and the Academy over, he returned from the 1940 Oscar ceremony at last united with the award he had refused four years earlier. He died in 1960, a Hollywood institution.

The First 'Blue Movie': Le Coucher de la Marie

It is a simple rule of life that, where technology leads, lumbering close up behind will be a man ready to use it to sell sex. This was certainly the pattern with cinema. In 1896, a mere year or so after the Lumière brothers had publicly shown their landmark motion picture, a fellow Frenchman, Eugène Pirou, produced *Le Coucher de la Marie* (*Bedtime for the Bride*).

Pirou, born sometime in the middle of the century, had long been keen on the evolving art of still photography, but that soon gave way to the possibilities offered by motion pictures in the 1890s. Early in 1896, he made an unsuccessful attempt to contact the Eastman

Kodak Company for further information about the Edison Vitascope (an early film camera). Instead, he turned to Henri Joly, another film pioneer who had invented a projector of his own, and started hosting a movie night at Paris's Café de la Paix in the spring of 1896. By the end of the year, he was making movies of his own.

The two titles to really establish his name could hardly have been more different. In October, he shot various scenes from the state visit to France of Czar Nikolas II of Russia, with Pirou subsequently marketing himself as 'Photographe des Rois'. Quite what His Imperial Majesty would have made of Pirou's other work undertaken at almost exactly the same time is anyone's guess. Having signed up the talents of a director known as Léar (real name Albert Kirchner and rumoured to have had a sideline in trading pornographic stills), he set about making *Le Coucher de la Marie*, a three-minute visual feast in which the impeccably name Louise Willy reproduced the show-stopping striptease that she had perfected for her famed stage shows. So was made the first great 'smoking-room' film.

This and the footage of the Czar proved huge hits when they premiered in Paris, and it was not long before Pirou had to arrange extra showings at two further venues in the city, as well as in Nice. By the beginning of

1897, it was on international release, although it was apparently withdrawn in London when shocked Victorian audiences complained. The film marked the start of a remarkable creative burst from Pirou, who completed some 50 movies before the end of 1897. After the turn of the century, though, he disappears from the historical record. As for Léar, he went on to make the first film based on the life of Jesus Christ.

The First Network Television Soap Opera:
Faraway Hill

The 'soap opera' was initially a creation of radio, developed to fill the daytime schedules and to appeal to an audience made up largely of housewives. A great many of these continuing dramas cropped up in the late 1920s and 1930s, often sponsored by soap companies such as Lever Brothers and Procter & Gamble (hence the 'soap' element of the genre name).

Television lagged somewhat behind radio in this period. The very first drama that can stake a claim as the 'first TV soap' was a 13-part series called *War Bride*. However, for its run in the summer of 1946, it was only broadcast on a local New York station. *Faraway Hill* was the first soap to be broadcast on a major network, the DuMont Network, premiering on 2 October 1946.

DuMont Laboratories had been founded in 1931 and

by the end of the decade it was a significant player in the television-set-manufacturing business. Its owner, Dr Allan DuMont, had also established a television station in New York that broadcast throughout the Second World War. Buoyed by the success of that initiative, he established a full-scale network in August 1946. However, unlike many of the other burgeoning television networks, DuMont had no background in radio. Because of this, he needed to build a creative base from scratch, having relatively little capital and no ready supply of established broadcasting stars to call on. In such circumstances, it was vital that he innovate. *Faraway Hill*, it was hoped, would be a key component of his network's programming.

Screened in black and white over half an hour on Wednesday evenings, the story revolved around the character of Karen St John, a widow from the Big Apple, who leaves her big-city life to set up home close to her relatives in a rural community. There she falls in love with the wrong man, and so the scene is set for a drama dealing with forbidden love as well as the tensions between urban and country life. It was produced by David P. Lewis, and the role of Karen was taken by Flora Campbell.

Unfortunately, though all the ingredients seemed in place for a success, the show failed to capture the imagination of viewers and it was cancelled after the end of its scheduled run, the last episode appearing on 18 December 1946. However, DuMont persevered with the model and another soap, *A Woman to Remember*, was broadcast on the network the following year. Over the ensuing years, DuMont came up with a number of winning formats and often featured in the charts of most-watched programmes. Nonetheless, it struggled to compete with its wealthier and longer-established broadcasting competitors and went out of business in 1956. Its legacy, though, lives on: in introducing the soap opera to television audiences, it helped establish one of the most popular and profitable of all television formats.

The First Million-Selling Record: 'Vesti la Giubba' by Enrico Caruso

Enrico Caruso is, arguably, the most famous opera singer to have ever lived. While this was principally down to the unerring quality of his tenor voice and his remarkable ability to convey emotion, his fame was certainly bolstered because he had the vision to record songs on to gramophone even when the technology was still in its infancy.

Born into a fairly impoverished family in Naples in 1873, Caruso took his professional bow at the city's Teatro

Nuovo in 1895, performing in a largely forgotten opera by Domenico Morelli. It was the start of a remarkable career that saw Caruso play at practically every great opera house in the world, including 18 seasons as the lead tenor at the New York Metropolitan Opera.

Whereas other famous singers of his age were wary of the nascent recording equipment then emerging, fearing (often correctly) that the technology would distort rather than enhance their renditions, Caruso embraced the opportunities it offered. He made his first recordings in Milan in late 1902 for the Gramophone & Typewriter Company (which would eventually become EMI). He was apparently paid the then grand fee of £100 for ten songs, to the disgust of some of the company's senior management. They need not have worried, for the tracks soon earned their money back.

Among this early batch of songs was 'Vesti la Giubba' ('On with the Motley'), the most memorable aria from Ruggero Leoncavallo's 1892 opera *Pagliacci*. It is performed by the character Canio as he readies himself to perform as the clown Pagliaccio, having just found out that his wife has been unfaithful. It is the classic 'tears of a clown' song, with lyrics including 'Laugh, Pagliaccio! / At your broken love. / Laugh at the grief that poisons your heart.' There really was no one better than Caruso to wring out the feeling.

It was a song he would record twice more, in 1904 and 1907. For the 1904 version and nine other songs, recorded on 1 February for Victor Records in the USA, he received a fee of $4,000. Performed with only a piano for backing (the 1907 recording would have a full orchestra), it was this version that became the first record to sell more than a million copies.

As the money rolled in for him and the record company, many of those performers previously reticent to allow their voices to be preserved in perpetuity now eagerly took up the gauntlet. Caruso himself recorded extensively while maintaining a draining schedule of live performance too. In 1920, the relentless pace began to tell and he suffered a devastating throat haemorrhage while on stage in New York. He made a few more live appearances but his body was now riven with infection and he died in his native Naples on 2 August 1921. His funeral was a virtual state occasion.

The First Casino: The Ridotto, Venice

Gambling may not be quite the oldest profession in the world, but it is probably not far off. For instance, we know that in ancient times eager gamblers rolled knucklebones in the fashion of modern dice. But, by and large, until the Renaissance gambling was an informal pastime, carried out between associates with a broadly equal risk of winning and losing.

However, things began to change in Europe around the fifteenth century with the growth in what has come to be known as *mercantile gambling*. A new system of gambling emerged whereby the game organiser (what we might term as *the house* today) made a calculation of the odds of winning and the payouts they could afford to make while ensuring that they came out on top over the long run. In the early sixteenth century, Venice was a particularly notable gambling hub, offering access to numerous lotteries until the city government decided it should protect the morals of the population by taking over the business for itself.

It has been suggested that, because Venice was a city-state whose fortunes were reliant on the vicissitudes of the sea and the weather, its people were temperamentally suited to gambling. So, when the lotteries were taken out of the private sphere, a great craze for mercantile dice and card games took its place. Although it was technically not legal, the authorities generally turned a blind eye, especially during the carnival months of October into March.

But by the second half of the 1500s, there was growing concern in government at the number of *ridotti* (private meeting rooms of the nobility) that were being turned over to gambling, complete with paid croupiers and often with huge stakes at risk. However, rather than outlaw these gambling dens, the Great Council of Venice decided in 1638 that there was much to be said for the old adage 'If you can't beat 'em, join 'em.'

So the Ridotto, the first state-licensed public casino in history, was opened in the San Moisa Palazzio of Marco Dandolo. While ostensibly open to anyone, in reality, this was a playground for the rich. That said, there was a cast of lowlife characters – from pimps and prostitutes to moneylenders and government informants – milling around in the background. On entering the Ridotto, patrons could partake of various sweet and savoury snacks and sate their thirst as well. Somewhat ironically for a place of vice, the main hall ceiling was adorned with a painting called *The Triumph of Virtue*. It is unclear who was trying to fool whom.

Gaming tables were run by Barnabots, a stratus of the nobility that had hit hard times, relying on parish handouts but unable to work because of their nominal high social status. Wearing long wigs and black gowns, they were, however, allowed to work at the casino, usually for a small salary. The gamblers themselves were expected to wear three-cornered hats and masks whenever they were actively playing, which could be pretty much all day from eight in the morning until the early hours. Vast fortunes were won and lost, with whole palaces being gambled on occasion. Regardless of what was at risk, it was not the done thing to show any emotion at the tables, whether of joy or despair.

The Great Council did very well out of its involvement, and the Ridotto was significantly expanded in the late 1660s using money taken from the city's convents. That redirecting of funds may have focused growing concern that the Ridotto was seriously impacting on the city's moral character, as well as dangerously reshaping its financial landscape. The decision to close it was taken by the Council on 27 November 1774 by an overwhelming majority of 720 to 21. Vice will have its way, though, and something like a hundred underground casinos sprang up to take its place.

The First Disc Jockey: Doc Herrold

In theory, it should be a relatively straightforward job to play a few songs on the radio and fill the gaps in between with a bit of idle chitchat. But, as anyone who has ever listened to 'the wireless' (as those of a certain age will still have it) will know, there are but a select few who really have a flair for it. Walter Winchell, an astute commentator on American life, was the first to use the term 'disc jockey' in 1935, referring to Martin Block, who had gained notoriety during the Charles Lindbergh kidnapping case by mixing the latest twists in the gripping news story with the newest records.

Retrospective glory as the first disc jockey was intense. Among the leading claimants was Reginald A. Fessenden, who was an electrical engineer employed by Thomas Edison. On 24 December 1906, he made a broadcast from Brant Rock, Massachusetts, during which he sang, played the violin, read from the Gospel of St Luke and spun a recording of a female singing 'Largo' by Handel.

While we must acknowledge that all of that must have made quite a show, it seems to have been something of a one-off. Next, then, we turn to Charles D. 'Doc' Herrold, a pioneer of the radio waves whose San Jose-based station began broadcasting (from a small farmstead) at the start of 1909. Herrold would later boast of personally installing crystal sets in houses throughout the local area in a bid to 'make my own audience'.

His assistant, Ray Newby, later recalled how they would shoot the breeze over whatever stories happened to be in that day's newspapers or any other subject of general interest that sprang to mind, in between playing popular tunes. All of which sounds very much like what the DJ of today might still expect to do. From 1912 until 1917 (when private parties were ordered off frequencies by the government), the station operated daily with a regular programming schedule, making it arguably the first radio station as we might recognise one now.

Herrold's wife, Sybil True, can also claim to be the world's first female disc jockey, regularly presenting *The Little Ham Program* from 1914 onwards. She ran weekly competitions offering enticing prizes to keep listeners coming back, amid a host of other thoroughly modern innovations. Proudly playing borrowed 'up-to-date, young people's records', Sybil's show was a boon to all the local record shops, who enjoyed much increased business for any discs she might have spun on the previous evening's show.

Unfortunately, the first couple on radio were not to last. With Sybil some 22 years younger than her husband, they decided to divorce in 1924. Charles's attempts at a commercially viable radio career faltered in that same decade and he was forced to take up several 'normal' jobs, including a stint as a dockyard janitor. He died in 1948.

The First Television Advertisement: Bulova Watches

The business of making television programmes is not a cheap one, and, from the earliest days of the medium,

TV executives were on the lookout for ways to bring in extra funding. It is, therefore, a little surprising that it was not until 1941 that the first paid-for advertisement was sent across the airwaves.

The company involved was the renowned Bulova Watch Company, based in the Queens area of New York. The company had been founded in 1875 by Joseph Bulova, an immigrant from Bohemia (in the modern-day Czech Republic). Dealing in precision clocks and watches, the company soon built a reputation for quality. In addition, he had a fine eye for a publicity opportunity. For instance, when the American president, Calvin Coolidge, presented 'Bucky' Harris, the manager of the 1924 World Series-winning Washington Senators, with a Bulova watch, Bulova marked the occasion with a new model of its own, 'the President'.

Two years later, it was Bulova who produced the first radio commercial in America, the same year as they offered a $1,000 prize for the first non-stop transatlantic flight. When Charles Lindbergh achieved the feat in 1927, Bulova produced a commemorative timepiece that sold some 50,000 units. According to the company's own accounts, in 1931 it became the first watch manufacturer to operate an advertising budget in excess of $1 million.

So it was hardly a shock when Bulova became the first

company to broadcast a TV advert just before 2.30pm on 1 July 1941. It appeared on the New York-based WNBT station in a break before a baseball game between the Brooklyn Dodgers and the Philadelphia Phillies, running for between 10 and 20 seconds and costing $9. It consisted of a map of the USA and a picture of one of the company's clocks, while a voiceover said, 'America runs on Bulova time.'

How successful it was in terms of new sales is difficult to gauge. What is certain is that such foresightedness, evident over a long period of time, did much to keep the Bulova name high in the American public's consciousness. Just how ahead of the game Bulova was becomes even clearer when one considers that it was a full 14 years before the first television advert appeared on British TV, a commercial for Gibbs S.R. toothpaste.

'You're a lucky man. We've just got in the new recliner with lumber support.'

CHAPTER TEN

Politics, Law and Order

The First First Lady: Dolley Madison

As everybody knows, George Washington was the first president of the USA (serving from 1789 to 1797) and so we might expect his wife, Martha, to have been the First Lady. Indeed, to all intents and purposes, she was, playing a supporting role to her husband and ably assisting him in welcoming visitors to the seat of government in New York and then Philadelphia (Congress relocated to Washington, DC, in 1800). However, it was a job she accepted with some resistance, once commenting, 'I am more like a state prisoner than anything else,' and that she would 'much rather be at home'.

The first presidential wife to be called First Lady was actually Dolley Payne Todd Madison, who was married to the fourth president, James Madison. While she did not receive the title until after her death in 1849 (in a funeral address by the incumbent president, Zachary Taylor), it was a position she filled not only for her own husband but also for his predecessor, Thomas Jefferson, who was a widower by the time he came to office.

Dolley was born on 20 May 1768 in North Carolina to strict, plantation-owning Quaker parents. In 1790, she married a fellow Quaker, a lawyer from Philadelphia by the name of John Todd Jr, with whom she had two sons. But tragedy was to strike just three years later, when John and one of the sons, William, died in a yellow-fever epidemic. She was a widowed single mother and still only 25.

Renowned for her beauty and vivaciousness, Dolley got through that tricky time and within a year was introduced by a friend to Madison, already well known for his role in drafting the US Constitution. Despite his being 17 years older than she, there was an immediate spark. They decided to marry and set up home on the Madison family pile in Orange County, Virginia. As he was an Episcopalian, Dolley found herself rejected by her fellow Quakers, but this seemed only to give freer rein to her naturally outgoing personality, and she became well known for her skills at entertaining, her daring outfits and the development of a snuff habit.

When Jefferson was elected president in 1801, he appointed Madison as his secretary of state, and Dolley suddenly found herself at the centre of Washington life. Without a wife of his own, the president asked her if she might act as hostess when required at the White House, something she managed with gusto. In 1808, it was her own husband being sworn in to the senior position, by which time she was well versed in what was required of her as his spouse. Where he seemed serious and stern, she was bright and engaging and her dinner parties were quite legendary.

She also proved her mettle when Washington came under attack from British troops during the War of 1812. She insisted on staying in the city until important documentation and artworks had been put into safekeeping. Eventually forced to flee, she returned after three days to discover the White House ransacked and burned. As ever, she dealt with the crisis brilliantly and showed the wider world a broad smile as she re-established normal life in the presidential home. Madison won re-election in 1812 and remained at the nation's helm until 1817.

The couple then returned to Orange County, where they lived out a happy retirement until James's death in 1836. Alas, her son from her first marriage, John Payne, was a rather dissolute character who rapidly worked his way through the family finances. Dolley sold the estate and returned to Washington, where she also had to sell many of her husband's papers to make ends meet. She was more loved than ever in the capital city and remained a stalwart of the social scene until her own death in July 1849, when her funeral was attended by huge crowds of well-wishers.

The First Serial Killer: Liu Pengli

The idea of the 'serial killer' – that is to say, a murderer who kills at least three victims in clearly distinct episodes without obvious motive – is a relatively modern one. It seems to have been first defined by Ernst Gennat, a German police officer and insightful criminologist, in 1930.

Germany had recently suffered two particularly notable serial killings. Fritz Haarmann had been convicted and executed for killing some 24 young men and boys between 1918 and 1924 in Hannover. Then Peter Kürten, 'The Vampire of Düsseldorf', went on a killing spree in 1929 that ended with his execution for nine murders and seven attempted murders. In an academic review of the cases, Gennat made use of the term 'Serienmörder'. The English-speaking world, though, was not to become familiar with the concept for several decades, until Robert Ressler, an FBI agent and significant figure in the history of criminal profiling, began using the term 'serial killer' in the 1970s.

But, just because we didn't have a name for it, it doesn't mean that it wasn't going on. The man (for it is usually men) who can be retrospectively identified as the first serial killer was Liu Pengli, a Chinese aristocrat who wreaked havoc for a good part of the second century BC.

According to the ancient historian Sima Qian, Liu Pengli was the cousin of the Han emperor Jing, and was crowned king of the Jidong area in 144 BC. Over a period of about 29 years, the ruler would gather together between 20 and 30 outlaws and ruffians to embark on marauding trips across the land, robbing and killing indiscriminately and at will. Word of Liu Pengli's atrocious deeds soon spread, but so terrified were his subjects that it took almost three decades before, finally, the son of one particular victim made a formal complaint to the emperor (by then Wu had succeeded his father Jing).

A thorough investigation was undertaken and it was discovered that Liu Pengli was responsible for the unlawful deaths of more than a hundred people. Court officials demanded that he be executed to satisfy the requirements of justice, but the emperor took pity on his blood relative, choosing instead to strip him of his privileges and send him into exile.

Several other serial killers have taken sport in killing despite the advantages that came to them through high birth. For instance, Gilles de Rais was a French knight found guilty of kidnapping and murdering anywhere from 80 to 600 peasant children in a life that lasted only 36 years in the first half of the fifteenth century. Then there was the Hungarian Countess Erzsébet Báthory, 'The Bloody Lady of Čachtice', who is believed to have tortured and killed several hundred girls and young women between 1590 and 1610. Clearly, bloodlust is no respecter of class.

The First International Peace Treaty:
Ramses II and Hattusilis III

Signed in 1258 BC, this was an agreement between Egypt and the Hittite Empire that ended decades of costly war. It was the first such agreement between major international powers and was remarkably modern in its formulation – so much so that a sculpted copy of it hangs in the United Nations headquarters in New York.

The Hittites emerged as a significant rival to Egypt, ruling over much of the territory that comprised Anatolia, and, in particular, the two powers rubbed up against each other in Syria. After several generations of decline, Egypt went through a grand renaissance under

Ramses, known as 'the Great', and was keen to flex its muscles in the region.

Tensions came to a head in about 1275 at the Battle of Kadesh, with Ramses intent on wresting control of the region back from the Hittites. Working on the basis of flawed intelligence (a problem that has beset leaders both ancient and modern), he expected to find the Hittites in fewer numbers than was actually the case. The result was a monumental chariot battle where the advantage swung from side to side. Both sides suffered huge casualties and in the end both claimed victory. History is still to decide who really came away with the advantage.

Animosity between the two sides inevitably festered but the prospect of further expensive battles appealed to no one, particularly in light of the fact that Egypt was also having to deal with the troublesome Libyans while the Hittites were under pressure from resurgent Assyria. So it was that negotiations began to strike a piece. After several years of diplomatic endeavour, agreement was reached in the 21st year of Ramses's rule (*circa* 1258 BC).

The treaty comprised 18 major clauses and was written in Egyptian hieroglyphs and in the ancient Babylonian Akkadian language. Under its terms, Egypt and the Hittite Empire declared that they would no longer fight each other and would recognise their mutually agreed borders. But the treaty went far beyond this in scope. It laid out a mutual defence agreement whereby either side would come to the aid of the other in the face of attacks from a third party, if requested. Both rulers could also be called on to help put down uprisings from within either power, again at the behest of their opposite number. Further provisions allowed for the arrest and return of fugitives or rebels fleeing from one power to the other. So not only was this the first peace treaty, but the first extradition pact as well.

To ensure the treaty was binding, both rulers swore to it, having invoked the gods as their witnesses and guarantors. There was but one discrepancy in the agreement as recorded by the Egyptian side and by the Hittite side – the Egyptians suggested that it had been Hattusilis who had sought the peace, while the Hittites maintained the initiative came from Ramses. Even in peace, boys will be boys ...

The First Man to Die in the Electric Chair: William Kemmler

The life of William Kemmler was not one of particular distinction. Its nadir came in March 1889, when the 29-year-old from Buffalo, New York, hacked to death his common-law wife, Tillie Ziegler, with a hatchet. He was convicted of the crime the following year, with the judge ruling that he be executed on 6 August 1890 in Auburn

Prison, New York. Kemmler's unseemly little life might have been consigned to history's footnotes were it not for the extraordinary battle that raged between two pioneers of the electricity industry, George Westinghouse and Thomas Edison. Instead, Kemmler found himself in the unenviable position of being the first man to die in the electric chair.

The feud between Westinghouse and Edison was the result of their fierce competition to power New York. Edison's Pearl Street power station lit up the financial and commercial districts of the city using direct current (DC), while George Westinghouse's company was illuminating Buffalo but using alternating current (AC). It was soon evident that AC was the superior system and Edison was confronted with falling sales.

Deciding that the best form of defence was attack, Edison set out to discredit the AC system. He hit upon the idea of persuading the public that the higher voltage required in AC posed an unacceptable risk to human life. He was ably supported in his mission by one Harold Brown, who was so keen to emphasise the dangers of AC that he executed an assortment of animals at public demonstrations to prove his point. He even challenged Westinghouse to an 'electric duel', suggesting that each of them be hooked up to his respective favoured current, with the power gradually increased to see which one screamed first. Westinghouse wisely declined the proposition.

At the same time, the State of New York was investigating new methods for executing convicted criminals after several botched hangings had fuelled public consternation. Edison addressed the commission charged with finding an alternative and convinced them that electricity (of the AC type, of course) was an efficient way to dispatch ne'er-do-wells. In 1888, the state administration wrote into law the use of electricity in executions and called on Brown to design a suitable method. His solution was the electric chair, a device he perfected in partnership with Arthur Kennelly. It was, Edison surely hoped, another step towards inextricably linking AC and death in the public imagination.

Kemmler was the unfortunate chosen to be the chair's first victim. With funding from Westinghouse, he appealed against his sentence on the basis that it was cruel and unusual and breached the Constitution, but to no avail. He woke early on the day of his execution, dressed smartly, breakfasted and prayed before arriving at 6.38am to face his end. 'See that things are right,' he told the attendants.

Alas, things were far from such (despite the fact that the chair had been tested successfully on a horse the day before). He was given an initial 17-second burst of high voltage, but it was clear to the throng gathered to witness the momentous event that he continued to breathe. A second blast went on for several minutes and was stopped only when the odour of charred flesh filled the air. From start to finish, Kemmler had taken eight minutes to die.

The *New York Herald* reported, 'The killing of Kemmler today marks, I fear, the beginning and the end of electrocution, and it wreathes in shame the ages of the great Empire State who, entrusted with the terrific responsibility of killing a man as a man was never killed before, brought to the task imperfect machinery and turned an execution into a horror.' Westinghouse apparently observed ruefully that 'they would have done better using an axe'. What Edison made of this unlikely outcome of his war on AC is not known.

The First Female Elected Head of Government: Sirimavo Bandaranaike

Sirimavo Bandaranaike served as prime minister of Sri Lanka three times between 1960 and 2000. Her first term, which lasted five years, came after she became the first woman to be democratically elected head of any government in the world. Her career, punctuated by assassin monks, uprisings and the imposition of emergency law, makes the tenure of Margaret Thatcher some 20 years later positively pale in comparison.

She was born Sirimavo Ratwatte in 1916, when Sri Lanka was still the British colonial possession of Ceylon, to a family who were landed, influential and Roman Catholic. After a convent education, she wed Solomon Bandaranaike in 1940, with both declaring their conversions to Buddhism.

Solomon was the founder of the Sri Lanka Freedom Party and their change of faith had distinct political undertones, as Buddhism was the religion of the majority Sinhalese population.

In 1948, Ceylon was granted dominion status within the British Commonwealth, and in 1956 Solomon was prime minister, pressing for Sinhalese rights at the expense of the Tamil minority, who he considered had received preferential treatment under the British. However, in September 1959, his life was brought to a premature end when he was shot by Talduwe Somarama, a Buddhist monk.

Sirimavo was persuaded to run as his replacement in the election of 1960, a campaign in which she became known as 'the Weeping Widow' for her regular tearful public appearances. In July of that year, she was duly elected and sworn in. However, if Ceylon was expecting her time to be marked by feminine gentleness, it was to experience something quite different. She continued her husband's pro-Sinhalese and anti-Tamil policies, which had already seen Sinhalese become the national language and which included positive discrimination in appointments to state-run businesses. With the Tamils agitating for greater recognition, and even a separate state, Sirimavo's justice minister (and also her nephew) memorably called for 'a little bit of totalitarianism'. When elections came round in 1965, Sirimavo lost the premiership.

However, she returned in 1970, as abrasive as ever. When a declining economic situation precipitated an uprising by students and activists in 1971, she responded by imposing emergency law for five years (presumably to her nephew's delight). In 1972, Sri Lanka was born out of Ceylon, with Buddhism as the state religion. In 1977, she was again ousted from power, leaving behind a disunited country, which now included the Tamil Tigers organisation. In 1980, she was banned from sitting in parliament and denied office for six years, having been found guilty of corruption while prime minister.

But there was still some governance left in her, and, when her daughter, Chandrika Bandaranaike Kumaratunga, was elected president in 1994, she reappointed her mother as premier, although the role wielded considerably less power than it had done in previous decades. Sirimavo stood down in 2000 and in October of that year, a few hours after casting her vote in the general election, she died from a heart attack.

The First Murderer to be Caught by Fingerprints: Francisca Rojas

Only rarely has the Argentine justice system led the world in progressiveness, but that was just the case when fingerprints were used for the first time to convict a mother of a particularly gruesome and brutal crime.

On 29 June 1892, Francisca Rojas emerged from her house, bleeding and screaming, in the coastal village of Necochea in the Buenos Aires province of the country. She had been attacked, she said, and her two children, a six-year-old boy and four-year-old girl, had been slaughtered, their throats cut. The man responsible, she told anyone willing to listen, was her neighbour, a rancher by the name of Pedro Ramón Velásquez. His apparent motive was her repudiation of his advances, although Velásquez vehemently denied any involvement and could provide a cast-iron alibi.

Nonetheless, he was taken into custody, where he was subjected to days of torture and was even tied up next to the corpses of the young victims in the hope that he would be shamed into a confession. He continued to plead his innocence and the case came to the attention of Juan Vucetich, a senior police officer who was a pioneering figure in the emerging field of fingerprinting and who the previous year had instituted a groundbreaking, comprehensive cataloguing system that allowed prints to be matched to suspects.

With nine days having passed since the crime was committed, he persuaded an investigating officer, Inspector Eduardo Alvarez, to go and reinspect the crime scene. Alvarez noticed a set of bloody fingerprints on the frame of a bedroom door and had the relevant section cut out and sent off for analysis. A study of the prints bore out the innocence of Velásquez, but revealed a perfect match with Rojas. Confronted with this damning evidence, the mother confessed. Her motivation for such an unspeakable deed was that she longed to marry another man who had indicated that he might assent were it not for the fact that he did not like children.

Velásquez was freed to return to his previously unremarkable life and Rojas went to trial in July 1892. As a woman she was exempt from the death sentence, but was found guilty and sentenced to a life term in prison instead. It was to be another decade before the first fingerprint murder conviction was secured in either Europe or North America.

The First Criminal Conviction by DNA:
Robert Melias

Less than a hundred years after the first fingerprint conviction, science had moved on so rapidly that the world was now talking in terms of *genetic fingerprints*. Investigators were now able to extract from crime scenes traces of DNA (material containing the basic genetic coding for all human life) and match it against samples from potential suspects. So reliable is the system that the chances of accidentally mismatching samples are several million to one.

The first case in which DNA evidence ensured a conviction was the trial of Robert Melias at Bristol Crown Court on 13 November 1987. Melias was a labourer from Avonmouth in Somerset with a long criminal record, mostly for burglary. It was alleged that on 29 January 1987 he broke into a house in his home town that belonged to a 43-year-old disabled woman. She was awoken by the noise of the break-in and was then confronted by Melias. He ordered her to lie face down on the bed and told her that he had an accomplice with him elsewhere in the building. Despite her protestations that she was disabled, he proceeded to rape her.

Police scientists were able to extract the DNA from semen found on the victim's clothes, which was sent for analysis at the Home Office's forensic-science laboratory in Aldermaston. When the suspect was initially questioned in connection with the incident, he denied any involvement but, apparently overcome by pangs of conscience, he submitted to a blood test, which uncovered the truth.

The odds that the DNA came from someone other than Melias were put at 4 million to one. Confronted with the incontrovertible evidence, he changed his plea to guilty two days before going to trial. Described by his defence barrister as a 'lonely, single man', Melias asked that five other burglaries, three separate offences and a breach of probation be taken into account. He was sentenced to eight years in prison.

Melias's trial was predated by a year by a curious case in which DNA was used for the first time in a high-profile investigation to *free* a suspect. In 1983, a 15-year-old girl, Lynda Mann, was raped and murdered in the Leicestershire village of Narborough. That was followed in 1986 by the rape and murder of another teen, Dawn Ashworth, at nearby Enderby. A 17-year-old kitchen hand called Rodney Buckland claimed responsibility for the Enderby crime, but not for the attack in Narborough, and was immediately taken into police custody.

Professor Alec Jeffreys at the University of Leicester

was at the forefront of the development of genetic fingerprinting and he proved categorically that the DNA found at the scene of both murders was from the same source, and that the source was not Buckland. Buckland was thus discharged at Leicester Magistrates' Court in November 1986. Colin Pitchfork was eventually caught and convicted of the crimes in 1988. He was the first murderer to be uncovered by a community-wide DNA screening programme (which he had initially managed to evade) and was also the first murderer to be convicted on DNA evidence. The reason for Buckland's false confession was never conclusively established.

The First State Passports: England, 1414

If we take a passport as being an officially recognised permission to travel across borders (international or not), then it may be assumed that they have existed in some form or other for as long as mankind has been able to communicate.

For instance, the Book of Nehemiah – the second of the Hebrew Bible and believed to date to the fifth century BC – includes a passage in which Nehemiah prepares to travel from Persia to Judea, having received from the king, Artaxerxes I, a letter requesting safe passage for his subject from governors of lands beyond his jurisdiction.

Later, Augustus Caesar (63 BC–AD 14) operated a

network of stations throughout the Roman Empire, whose amenities could be accessed by him, any of his men or any official given explicit authorisation via a *tractorium*. This was typically a tablet inscribed with the name of the emperor administering it, the name of the official holding it and the length of time for which it was valid (or until the death of the authorising emperor, if that date came first).

There is also ample evidence of 'safe conduct' documents being issued by Edward the Confessor and William of Normandy in England in the eleventh century, with certain of those not possessing them being refused entry. Indeed, the Magna Carta, signed by King John in 1215, included a clause thus:

> It shall be lawful for the time to come for anyone to go out to our kingdom and return safely and securely by land or water, saving his allegiance to us unless in time of war for some short space for the common benefit of the kingdom, except prisoners and outlaws and people in wars with us and merchants who shall be in such condition as is above mentioned.

Which rather seems to be suggesting that the king do away with any passport system he may have in mind.

However, for all of this, the first legislative enshrining of the passport did not come until 1414, during the reign of Henry V. Whereas the other mechanisms mentioned above were employed on something of an *ad hoc* basis, Henry's 'Safe Conducts' represented the first concerted effort to provide subjects with a way of proving their identity while in foreign climes. They were, in effect, a threat from the royal personage himself to any Johnny Foreigner who might be thinking of obstructing the journey of one of his citizens.

Granted for limited time periods (usually covering a single trip), they of course lacked any technological devices such as photographs or microchips. However, they did contain a description of the holder in a bid to head off fraudulent use. One can only imagine the havoc caused should a traveller have decided to change his hairstyle, or have gained a little weight around the jowls or, worse still, found himself *sans* a limb or two after an accident en route.

The First Woman Voter: Lilly Maxwell

New Zealand was the first nation to grant the vote to women in parliamentary elections, doing so in 1893. Conversely, in Britain, the 1832 Reform Act had specifically outlawed women from voting and it would not be until 1928 that there was universal suffrage. So how did it come about that Lilly Maxwell, a mild-mannered and otherwise quite un-notable lady from Manchester, became the first woman to vote in a parliamentary election anywhere in the world all the way back in 1867?

Lilly's exact birth date is not known but it is believed she was born in Scotland around 1800. As for a great many Victorian women not fortunate enough to have been born into wealth, she spent the greater part of her working life in domestic service, predominantly around the great commercial city of Manchester. For many years, she was in the employ of the Leech family, whose number included Sir Bosdin Thomas Leech, who gained fame as a driving force behind the Manchester Ship Canal.

At some point in the first half of the 1860s, Lilly retired from domestic service and set up in business as the manager of a modest crockery shop. The shop no doubt gave Lilly, a widow, a vital regular income in her later years. Then, in November 1867, Lilly found herself unexpectedly, and briefly, a figure of national interest.

The incumbent Member of Parliament in Manchester had passed away so a by-election was called. Only a few months earlier the Second Reform Act had been passed, extending the vote to any man who paid rates. While Lilly was herself a ratepayer, there was no getting away from the fact that in certain other vital respects she did not fulfil the criteria to have a say in who should be the next MP. Yet by some administrative glitch, her name (misspelled as Lily) was included on the electoral roll.

This clerical oversight came to the attention of the Liberal candidate, Jacob Bright, who passed on the news to Lydia Baker, a prominent member of the slowly blooming women's suffrage movement. Lilly was apparently initially reluctant to make a spectacle of herself but held her own firm views on women's rights and was eventually persuaded to go to the polling station, where voting was still by public declaration. With her name on the electoral register for all to see, the returning officer was obliged to note her selection, which was greeted by a spontaneous burst of applause from those present. Bright was elected MP with a clear and unambiguous majority, so Lilly's vote went unchallenged in the courts.

Discussing the question of votes for women with *The Times* in the aftermath of his election, Bright noted that Lilly was an honest, hardworking ratepayer. 'If any person should possess a vote,' he ruminated, 'it is precisely such as she.' The MP would himself go on to suggest an amendment to the 1869 Municipal Corporations Act, allowing female householders to vote in British municipal elections for the first time.

Alas for Lilly, her moment in the limelight was followed by steady decline. Her finances dwindled and she was forced back into service, this time as a charwoman. In April 1876, she entered the workhouse in Withington, a suburb of Manchester, where she died six months later from a combination of bronchial and gastric complaints.

'He compiled the first crossword.'

CHAPTER ELEVEN
A Final Miscellany

The First Roller-Skater: John Joseph Merlin

It is often said that there is but a thin line between genius and madness, and that maxim is backed up by the behaviour of Belgian John Joseph Merlin, who achieved much in his life. It included convincing himself that travelling on foot could be improved by attaching dangerously unstable wheels to his extremities.

Born on 17 September 1735 in Huys, Belgium, he moved to Paris as a young man to begin life as a maker of clocks and precision instruments. It was a business at which he absolutely excelled. Not only were his clocks and watches regarded as among the best available, he dedicated much time to the development of a 'perpetual-motion machine' (which relied on atmospheric pressure changes), designed weighing machines and wheelchairs, and improved on traditional musical instruments, such as the harpsichord. An overachiever in so many areas, Merlin was a most proficient exponent of the harpsichord and the violin in his own right. Eventually, there would even be a Mechanical Museum to display the many creations born from his magnificent mind.

It was inevitable that the fame of such a polymath would spread, and in 1760 Merlin was summoned to London at the request of the Spanish ambassador. The boy from the Belgian backwaters seems to have thrown himself wholeheartedly into the capital's metropolitan lifestyle and soon counted among his friends the likes of Bach, Horace Walpole and Gainsborough, who painted Merlin's portrait.

It was in this period that Merlin hit upon the idea of the roller-skate. After some experimentation, he decided the best approach was to attach two wheels to a metal plate, which could then be tied to the wearer's shoes with leather straps. They were in all major aspects an early version of the modern inline skate. It is not known how much time Merlin spent practising with this new equipment. The suspicion is that it wasn't long enough. Things were to come to a head when he was invited to a masked ball at Carlisle House in the very fancy Soho Square area of London.

Perhaps Merlin was feeling nervous in such a grand social setting or perhaps he had been rather over-enthusiastic in tucking into the fine wines on offer. Whatever the reason, at some point his brilliant brain calculated that it would be a good idea to emerge into the ballroom, playing the violin while roller-skating. It might, one could suppose, have been his crowning moment had it come off. In reality, he lost his footing, careered into a hugely expensive mirror, destroyed the violin he was carrying and left himself badly bruised and shaking. In addition, it put back the cause of the roller-skate by several decades. For the rest of us, though, it is perhaps reassuring to know that even the greatest can't be good at everything.

The First Teddy Bear Manufacturers: Morris and Rose Michtom

Around 40 per cent of American adults are in possession of a teddy bear that they owned as a child. Teddy bears have become a shorthand symbol for childhood innocence itself. And, as everyone knows, they got their name from Theodore 'Teddy' Roosevelt, president of the USA from 1901 to 1903. Quite an achievement for a man who in reality enjoyed few things as much as hunting animals.

For this strange twist in the tale, we have to thank two immigrants, shopkeepers Morris and Rose Michtom, who had fled the pogroms of Russia for the safety of New York in the 1880s. By that point cuddly bears were already commercially available but had failed to capture the public's imagination. Their most famous creator was Margarete Steiff, a woman from Giengen in Germany who had been wheelchair-bound since a childhood bout of polio. She used her impressive skills as a seamstress to make a living and created her first stuffed bear around 1880. This, though, was little more than a sideline and certainly did not turn her into a rich woman for many years.

The story of the 'teddy bear' does not begin until 1902, when Roosevelt was invited to adjudicate on a boundary dispute between the states of Louisiana and Mississippi. The president decided to make an event of the trip, so pencilled in five days for a black-bear hunt. Pursued by an eager pack of journalists, Roosevelt had met with a singular lack of success by day four and it was starting to get embarrassing. On the final day, one of his group did what they presumably thought was the decent thing, chased down an ageing bear with hounds, clubbed it and then tied it to a tree, ready for Roosevelt to dispatch it. But Teddy would have none of it. No way would he shoot a defenceless animal. It had to at least have a sporting chance. He put away his gun, although he did order that the distraught and exhausted creature be mercifully put out of its misery.

The famous cartoonist Clifford Berryman seized upon

the incident for the next day's newspaper and depicted the president turning away from the entrapped beast. For a knowing audience, it had clear political undertones in light of Roosevelt's dinner with the black political leader Booker T. Washington a year earlier. Roosevelt had been subject to a backlash from certain sections of the population, outraged that he would entertain such a man at the heart of government. The cartoon clearly reflected this situation in its depiction of a white man in the Southern States tying a black bear to a tree while the president looked away in disgust. However, where the original cartoon featured a fully grown animal, it was reproduced over the following days with a cute little cub in its place. The president won huge public acclaim for his decency towards the creature in the circumstances.

Meanwhile, in Brooklyn, the Michtoms were struggling along with their candy store when Morris had an idea. He suggested Rose make a cuddly bear just like the little one in the cartoon. She made two, which they marketed in the store as 'Teddy's Bear'. Thirteen people enquired about buying them, so Morris persuaded Rose to up production. He sent the original bear to the president in Washington and enquired as to whether they could use the name. Roosevelt famously responded, 'I don't think my name is likely to be worth much in the toy bear business but you are welcome to it.'

By early 1903, the Michtoms' bears were selling in vast numbers. They closed down their store and founded the Ideal Novelty & Toy Co., which remained in the family until the 1970s. Miss Steiff back in Germany also benefited when an American entrepreneur ordered 3,000 of her bears (now considered the gold standard among collectors) for import. Nor would Roosevelt miss out on the buzz. He had teddy bears present at all the stops on his successful 1904 presidential trail.

The First Man to Tightrope-Walk Across Niagara Falls: The Great Blondin

Emile Gravelet Blondin was born in St Omer, France, in 1824 and was the greatest funambulist (that is, tightrope walker) of his age. He received the moniker 'The Great Blondin' on account of his eye-catching mop of blond hair. In a business where the big bucks were in ever more incredible feats of daring, he became the first man across Niagara, a performance he repeated many times over a two-year period with ever more extraordinary twists.

Blondin was only five when he made his debut as an acrobat, billed as 'The Little Wonder'. In the mid-1850s, he took up the offer of an engagement with New York's Ravel troupe and became a favourite on the American circus scene. However, he was hungry for greater glory and developed an obsession with tackling the dangers represented by Niagara. 'To cross the roaring waters became the ambition of my life,' he would later recall.

After much preparation, he was ready to make his first attempt on 30 June 1859. At a little after 5pm, dressed in a black wig, purple vest and his customary white tights, he set off from the New York side of the gorge, carrying a 9-metre-long (30-foot) balancing pole to help him along the wire. He was to travel some 365 metres (1,200 feet) on the wire, which measured a little over 7.5 centimetres (3 inches) in diameter and hung suspended more than 45 metres (150 feet) above the raging waters.

Watched by a large and tense crowd of between 5,000 and 10,000, he began to move his wiry 1.6-metre (5 foot 5 inch) frame across the gorge. At the halfway point, he stopped for a breather, dropping a rope down to the famous *Maid of the Mist* tourist boat below to obtain a bottle of water, from which he drank heartily as the audience looked on astounded. He then continued with the rest of the crossing (which was now uphill, as the rope sagged in the middle) and made it to Canadian territory after 17 minutes. It was then reported that he drank a celebratory glass of champagne, danced a jig of joy on the rope and made the return crossing in less than half the time it had taken him on the way there.

Such was the interest in his achievement, not to say the potential for more earnings, that Blondin arranged another crossing for 4 July. On that occasion, he spiced up the event with some outrageous acrobatics on the wire and by making the return trip under a large sack that reached all the way to his knees, leaving him unsighted and severely restricted in movement. He continued to perform the walk throughout the rest of that summer and the following one, too. On different occasions he made the crossing in the dark, pushing a wheelbarrow, jumping somersaults and, perhaps most famously of all, carrying his manager, Harry Colcord, on his shoulders.

He made his 17th and last Niagara crossing on 8 September 1860, this time carrying a chair on which he sat mid-journey to drink some bubbly and have a slice of cake. He subsequently moved to England and set up home in London, though he continued to tour extensively throughout Europe. He wowed the public with his derring-do until a year before he died in 1897. To the world at large he was an incredible and brave entertainer. However, it should be noted that Mark Twain was less enamoured by his antics, describing him only as 'that adventurous ass'.

The First Recipient of the Victoria Cross:
Charles Lucas

The bloody battlefields of the Crimean War provided the backdrop for many acts of astonishing bravery. In such circumstances, the British ruling class came to acknowledge the need for a medal that recognised gallantry in the crucible of war regardless of rank. Thus, it was decided to institute a new medal, the Victoria Cross, to be awarded 'to those officers or men who have served Us in the presence of the Enemy and shall then have performed some signal act of valour or devotion to their country'.

The medals were cast by the jewellery firm Hancocks of Bruton Street from the metal of Russian guns captured in the Crimea. The first ceremony to bestow the award (which came with a £10 pension) was arranged for 26 June 1857, when Queen Victoria was to honour 62 recipients from horseback in London's Hyde Park.

Charles Lucas was the first man to be awarded the Victoria Cross, for his conduct on HMS *Hecla*. Lucas had been born into a land-owning family in County Armagh in 1834 and signed up with the Navy when just 14 years old. His first action came in 1852 during the Second Burmese War. By the outbreak of war with Russia in 1854, Midshipman Lucas had been assigned to the lightly armoured steam ship *Hecla*, which was charged with making reconnaissance missions into the Baltic. This she did successfully under the captaincy of one William Hall, before joining up with the rest of the

British fleet back at Dover and then returning to the theatre of war.

The Russian Navy was not keen to engage and *Hecla* bided her time, bar the odd small skirmish. Perhaps Hall was itching to get stuck in because on 21 June 1854 *Hecla* and two other ships began a bombardment of the Bomarsund fortress, off the Finnish coast. It was, in truth, an attack those particular vessels were ill suited to undertake, and before long the heavyweight fortress guns were returning fire. As a result, a live shell, complete with burning fuse, found its way on to *Hecla*'s upper deck. The order went up for every man in the crew to hit the deck for his own safety.

Lucas – still only 20, let us not forget – ignored the command and showed remarkable presence of mind and startling courage. He picked up the shell, ran to the ship's side and flung it into the sea. It exploded with an almighty bang before even touching the water, but *Hecla* was left with only cosmetic damage, and just two men suffered minor injuries. Captain Hall promoted Lucas to acting lieutenant there and then and also wrote to Vice-Admiral Charles Napier to recommend his young colleague's conduct (while himself receiving a dusting-down for his reckless captaincy).

Though Lucas's actions were the earliest to win a Victoria Cross, he was actually fourth in line to meet the Queen at the 1857 investiture. Nonetheless, he has gone down in the historical record as the first recipient. He retired from the Navy in 1873, having achieved the rank of captain and lived out an active retirement (including stints as a justice of the peace) in Kent. In 1885, he was made a retired rear-admiral. He died peacefully in August 1914, just as the world was about to enter a new era of terrible ferocity, punctuated by still more acts of inspiring bravery.

The First Christmas Card Sender: Sir Henry Cole

Henry Cole was a true product of the Victorian age, imbued with a sharp commercial sense balanced by a love of culture and a sense of duty towards the wider society. A favourite of Queen Victoria and, even more so, Prince Albert, he helped reshape the cultural landscape of London. But perhaps no contribution of his has proved to be so long-lastingly and widely popular as his creation of the commercial Christmas card.

Born in Bath in 1808, Cole began working for the Public Record Office when just 15, rising to become assistant keeper of the records and being credited with instigating a host of efficiency reforms. Then, from 1837 to 1840, he worked as the assistant to Rowland Hill, in which role he played a crucial part in the establishment of the penny-post service.

Ironically for a man who did so much to improve the

means of communication between people, he found he had less and less time for correspondence with his friends and loved ones. With this in mind, in 1843, he approached a renowned Devon-based illustrator (and later rector of the Royal Academy), John Callcott Horsley, to design a card offering pre-printed seasonal greetings, which he could simply sign and send.

Horsley came up with a triptych design. A panel on the left showed a scene of the poor being fed; on the right the naked were being clothed; and in the centre a family group raised glasses of wine to celebrate the Christmas spirit. The card proved immensely popular with its recipients and so Cole decided to print some commercially, which he could then sell through a shop on Old Bond Street.

The only people who seemed less keen were certain temperance groups, who objected to the great Christian feast being celebrated with the drinking of alcohol. It must have been a surprise for Horsley to find himself criticised for loose morals, as he was among the most prudish in an age of prudishness, campaigning over many years against the use and depiction of nude models in the art world. For this stance, he came to be known as 'Clothes Horsley'.

Nonetheless, most of your average, buttoned-up Victorians saw nothing wrong with the depiction on the Christmas card and enjoyed the simple sentiment it carried: 'A Merry Christmas and a Happy New Year to You'. Two batches of some thousand cards each flew out of the shop at a shilling (5p) each. Fewer than a dozen are known to have survived and, when one, sent to a Miss Mary Tripsack by persons unknown, was put up for auction in 2005, it commanded an inflation-busting £8,469.

In 1851, Cole was a crucial figure in the organisation of the hugely successful Great Exhibition. Afterwards, he helped transform South Kensington into one of the world's great cultural hubs, serving as the first director of the South Kensington Museum (later renamed the Victoria & Albert Museum) and assisting in the establishment of such notable institutions as the Royal College of Art and the National Training Schools for Music and Cookery. For his work, he was knighted in 1875, an honour he accepted only when Prime Minister Benjamin Disraeli assured him that Queen Victoria was especially insistent on the issue. She was, we must suspect, the person at the very top of his Christmas card list.

The First Woman to Wear a Bikini:
Micheline Bernardini

'A bikini,' the American wit Joey Adams once noted, 'is like a barbed-wire fence. It protects the property without obstructing the view.' From Marilyn Monroe, Ursula Andress and Brigitte Bardot to Raquel Welch, Elle Macpherson and Halle Berry, the bikini has occupied a unique place in our culture, at once daring, sexy and carefree. Yet, when it first hit the catwalks in 1946, it was a job to find a model prepared to sport one. That was until the game Micheline Bernardini turned up, a girl for whom excessive modesty was not a noticeable characteristic.

The designer of the teeny-weeny, itsy-bitsy beachwear was Louis Réard, born in France in 1897 and an automobile engineer by training. However, by the 1940s, the large part of his working life was spent running his mother's fashion outlet in Paris. It is surely no coincidence that his most famous creation came just after the end of the Second World War, when Western Europe could once again begin to embrace the frivolous. While the two-piece swimming cossie was not a new invention, Réard's designs of 1946 offered an unprecedented risqué factor. Having found himself in something of a battle with another Parisian designer, Jacques Heim, who claimed his 'Atom' creation was 'the world's smallest bathing suit', Réard hit back with a design he marketed as 'smaller than the smallest swimsuit'.

Indeed it was, created from just 177 square centimetres (27½ square inches) of fabric, exposing for all the world the wearer's belly button (officially classified as 'indecent' in the Hollywood film industry's Hays Code of the time) and a high-cut G-string brief that left little to the imagination. It should not be forgotten that only 45 years had passed since the death of Queen Victoria, in whose reign it was thought appalling for a lady to display even a glimpse of ankle.

Réard knew his garment would prove a sensation. He named it the bikini after the Pacific Atoll where the Americans had just tested an atomic bomb. It was perhaps a wry acknowledgement that any woman wearing one could expect to cause similar shockwaves. The only problem was, he could not find an established model brave enough to run the gauntlet of potential criticism by being the first to wear one in public. Then along came Mlle Bernardini, only 19 years old and up to that point making her living by 'dancing exotically' at the Casino de Paris, where she was accustomed to exposing more than even the bikini revealed.

So, on 5 July 1946, she donned Réard's little number, which was printed with a newspaper-print design. She appeared at a Paris swimming pool, Piscine Molitor, where she was photographed extensively. Even in those black-and-white photos, you can spot that Bernardini was not used to being outside in such a skimpy outfit as she revealed a pale line across her back and distinctly white buttocks, areas that normally went unsunned in the more robust swimming suits worn up till then.

Unfortunate tanning lines aside, the bikini got the sort of response Réard must have dreamed of. The Vatican came out in protest and it was initially banned by a swathe of southern European nations. Even *Vogue* took a rather snotty attitude, complaining that certain coastlines were resembling 'the backstage of music halls'. While sales took a while to spike, people soon got used to the idea of flashing the flesh, especially when Hollywood starlets began to pave the way. While other designers copied Réard's designs, he insisted that the test of a true bikini was whether it could be pulled clean through a wedding ring. As for Micheline, she proved Cole Porter's assertion that anything now went and received 50,000 letters from fans, no doubt some of them offering to rub in tanning lotion on those pasty bits.

The First Crossword Compiler: Arthur Wynne

For a certain section of the world, the crossword is simply the most diverting thing you can do on your own and with your clothes on. The first one was created by Arthur Wynne and appeared in the 'Fun' section of the *New York World* on 21 December 1913.

Born on 22 June 1871 in the Everton area of Liverpool, Wynne was the son of the editor of the *Liverpool Courier*. He left for a new life in the USA in his twenties, initially finding employment on a Texan onion farm. However, newspapers were in his genes and it was not long before he got a job editing the society section of a publication in, ironically, Liverpool, Ohio. From there, he found his way to Pennsylvania, turning his journalistic hand to whatever subject was thrown at him (as well as moonlighting as a violinist with the Pittsburgh Philharmonic for a while).

Then came the call from the Big Apple, where he was asked to edit the puzzles section of the *New York World*, which published every Sunday. A great lover of quizzes, he took the job with glee. After a while, he had the idea of reviving a word game from his childhood, which involved the arrangement of a given set of words into a grid so that the letters read the same both down and across. Mulling this over, he came up with a variant he called 'Word-Cross', played in a diamond-shaped grid, with a clue to each of the 32 words to be entered on to it.

The readers were grabbed as soon as it was published on that Sunday in December. Clues ranged from the simplistic (1 Down: To govern; Answer: RULE) to the distinctly tricky (10 Down: The fibre of the gomuti palm; Answer: DOH). Another one (18 Across: What this puzzle is; Answer: HARD) may even qualify as the world's first postmodern crossword clue.

Letters poured in to praise the new game, and over the next few months Wynne played with the format, trying out different grid shapes, before settling on the classic square and eventually renaming it the 'Cross-word'. By 1914, he was able to publish several puzzles devised and sent in by fans, and within a few years other papers were publishing their own crosswords.

However, the craze did not go into overdrive until 1924, when two graduates of the Columbia School of Journalism called Dick Simon and Lincoln Schuster published a volume of the *New York World*'s quizzes under their new imprint, Simon & Schuster. Most were devised not by Wynne himself but his successor on the 'Fun' section, Margaret Petheridge.

With that book hitting sales in excess of 2 million, crosswording spread like wildfire. The *Sunday Express* became the first British paper to run puzzles regularly (adapting Wynne's little gems in the early days), but not everyone was a fan. The *New York Times* took a most sniffy tone in condemning the 'sinful waste in the utterly futile finding of words the letters of which will fit into a prearranged pattern'. It was not until 1942 that its editor finally caved in and joined virtually every other newspaper in the land by including a crossword for the pleasure of its readers.

Having never patented his idea, Wynne did not reap the huge financial rewards that might have been expected from such a worldwide phenomenon. Nonetheless, he led a comfortable and contented life, which ended in a hospital in Clearwater, Florida, in January 1945.

The First Beauty Pageant Organiser:
P. T. Barnum

For many of us, the beauty pageant with its focus on assumed ideals of physical beauty is an anachronistic concept in the twenty-first century. It is interesting to note that even P. T. Barnum, arguably the greatest showman who ever lived, failed to win widespread support for the very first beauty contest, though for rather different reasons.

Phineas Taylor Barnum was born on 5 July 1810 in Connecticut and started out in newspapers before moving to New York to begin a career in show business. He made a fortune by drawing on his newsman experience to create excitement over whatever the current curiosity was that he wanted to charge the public to see. So it was that he could attract colossal crowds to gawp at 'human mermaids', tattooed men, dwarves, 'man-monkeys' and Siamese twins (to give a short selection from a very long list).

While Victorian society was quite at home enjoying a 'freak show', it was not yet ready to embrace the beauty pageant when he tried to sell the idea in 1854. Having already had success with a variety of other beauty contests, in which babies, flowers or dogs were all judged on their aesthetics, he no doubt considered it a natural step to reimagine such a contest for women. The prizes were impressive, too: a diamond tiara if the winner was married and an unspecified 'dowry' if she was single. Had it taken off, it would have given wonderful publicity to his other enterprises.

But, as things turned out, the world would not countenance such public scrutiny of the female form. Voyeurism was clearly acceptable on some level but only up to the point where sexuality was not explicit. Not only did commentators react to the announcement of the contest with howls of moral outrage, but also it seemed no respectable girl would consider entering, regardless of the rewards on offer. Barnum found himself with a roll-call of entrants who were described politely as of 'questionable reputations'. Barnum was nothing if not responsive to the public mood, and promptly pulled the competition.

He, of course, recovered from the setback. While no good girl would dream of parading herself in public, he discovered that they might submit tasteful daguerreotypes of themselves for publication and consideration in the newspapers. The press barons lapped up this development and ran newspaper beauty contests well into the twentieth century. So, from the clutches of disaster, Barnum had rescued the concept and found a way to spin some money out of it, too.

In truth, though, the 1850s were not Barnum's greatest decade, due in large part to several ill-considered financial investments. However, his fortunes took a turn for the better in the 1860s, when he started touring his famous circus, 'The Greatest Show on Earth'. In addition, he became, perhaps surprisingly, a keen temperance advocate as well as a member of the Connecticut legislature. He died a legend in 1891, a few years too soon to see the beauty pageant become a popular fixture in respectable American (and international) life and long before the rise of feminism again called into question its social validity. All those sweethearts dressed in their skimpies and claiming to want to save the world or look after sick kittens owe a debt of gratitude to him.

The First Nobel Peace Prize Winners: Frédéric Passy and Henry Dunant

Alfred Nobel was the inventor of dynamite and, when his brother died, a newspaper accidentally published an obituary of Alfred instead. It described him as 'an angel of death' on account of his explosive creation and awakened within him a great fear that his life would be remembered as a destructive rather than constructive one. So he established a fund in his will to establish the prizes that bear his name. The joint winners of the first Peace Prize, awarded in 1901, were Frédéric Passy and Henry Dunant, whose lives followed vastly different paths.

Passy, who was born in Paris in 1822, qualified as a lawyer and began a career in the civil service before giving himself up entirely to the study of economics. A great believer in the creed of free trade, he concluded that it offered the best chance of lasting peace as nations gave up their weapons to protect their shared commercial interests. While his academic reputation grew, he also developed a number of practical initiatives as well. With Franco-Prussian relations straining over the fate of Luxembourg in the 1860s, he established the Independent and Permanent League of Peace. When France and Prussia went to war in 1870, he dissolved the League and founded the French Society for the Friends of Peace, which itself evolved into the French Society for Arbitration between Nations.

Between 1881 and 1889, Passy sat in the French Chamber of Deputies, where he did much work to promote international peace. Inspired by the arguments of Randal Cremer in Britain, who had established an arbitration system to resolve disputes between the UK and the USA, in 1889 Passy became one of three presidents of the Interparliamentary Union (which still exists today), an organisation that sought to secure peace between nations when normal diplomatic avenues failed. After receiving his Nobel Prize for a lifetime's work, he continued to write and teach, spreading his ideas until his death in 1912.

In comparison, the life of his co-winner Dunant was rather more erratic. Born into a well-respected family in Geneva in 1828, he entered the commercial world as a young man and travelled extensively in a professional capacity. The turning point of his life came around 1861, when he hit upon a scheme to make a fortune out of a large area of land in Algeria. However, for his plan to come to fruition, he needed to establish water rights, and for that he required the assent of Napoleon III. At that time, the emperor was waging a military campaign in Italy but, undeterred, Dunant decided to appeal to him in person.

It came to pass that he caught up with Napoleon in the immediate aftermath of the bloody battle of Solferino, an event inspiring a book by Dunant the following year. Struck by the 'despair unspeakable, and misery of every kind', he described the efforts to look after the war wounded and laid out a vision for an international voluntary body that could care for those injured in war without fear of attack themselves. Dunant was subsequently asked to join a committee to investigate the practicalities of his idea, which led to the signing of the Geneva Convention in 1864 and the establishment of the Red Cross.

Yet, by 1867, Dunant was to enter a period of life in which he was all but forgotten. Having devoted himself to good works, he had neglected his commercial interests. His company set up to oversee the Algerian project went bankrupt, costing many of his Geneva associates their wealth. *Persona non grata* in his city of birth, he lived as a vagrant. Eventually, he ended up in a hospice in the Swiss village of Heiden. He was then 'rediscovered' by academics and journalists in the 1890s and received numerous honours and prizes worth a considerable amount of money (not the least of which was the Nobel Prize). Yet he lived out the remainder of his life in the hospice, before his death in 1910. He left some money to those who had cared for him and the bulk of his fortune to philanthropic organisations, while he himself was buried without ceremony in accordance with the terms of his will.